THE 21ST CENTURY
ORGANIZATION

Reinventing Through Reengineering

Warren Bennis & Michael Mische

The Jossey-Bass Business & Management Series

Jossey-Bass Publishers • San Francisco

The excerpt from "Reengineering: Out of the Rubble" by S. Greengard from *Personnel Journal*, Dec. 1993 is used by permission of ACC Communications Inc./ Workforce, Costa Mesa, CA. Copyright © December 1993. All rights reserved.

FIRST PAPERBACK EDITION PUBLISHED IN 1997.
THIS BOOK WAS ORIGINALLY PUBLISHED BY PFEIFFER & COMPANY.

Substantial discounts on bulk quantities of Jossey-Bass books are available to corporations, professional associations, and other organizations. For details and discount information, contact the special sales department at Jossey-Bass Inc., Publishers (415) 433-1740; Fax (800) 605-2665.

For sales outside the United States, please contact your local Simon & Schuster International office.

Jossey-Bass Web address: http://www.josseybass.com

Cover Design: Paul Bond
Interior Design, Page Composition, Illustrations: Lee Ann Hubbard
Editor: Carol Nolde
Editorial Assistant: Susan Rachmeler
Production Editor: Dawn Kilgore

 Manufactured in the United States of America on Lyons Falls Turin Book. This paper is acid-free and 100 percent totally chlorine-free.

Library of Congress Cataloging-in-Publication Data

Bennis, Warren G.
  The 21st Century organization : reinventing through reengineering
  / Warren Bennis & Michael Mische.
    p.   cm. — (Warren Bennis executive briefing series)
  Includes index.
  ISBN: 0-89384-273-7 (hardcover)
  ISBN: 0-7879-0939-4 (paperback)

  1. Organizational change.   2. Corporate reorganizations.
  I. Mische, Michael.   II. Title.   III. Title: Twenty-first century organization
  IV. Series
  HD58.8.B4623   1995
  658.4' 063—dc20   95-16196

FIRST EDITION
HB Printing   10 9 8 7 6 5 4 3 2 1
PB Printing   10 9 8 7 6 5 4 3 2 1

Dedication

To our loving wives and families,
who have taught us so much.

Contents

Editor's Preface

There are enormous and irreversible changes sweeping through the world today. These changes are redefining the ways in which people work and interact with one another. In fact, change is happening so quickly that leaders of both private and public organizations are finding that they face a constant and bewildering barrage of challenges. Successfully meeting such challenges will require new methods, new skills, new structures—in short, a new organization.

Reinventing today's organization to meet the challenges of the 21st Century is the subject of this book. Despite the popularity of reinventing—or reengineering—this difficult topic is confusing to many. Consequently, I am pleased to have coauthored this book with my colleague and friend, Michael A. Mische, whose extensive experience in leading organizations through the process of reengineering proved invaluable in clarifying the process for readers.

Michael and I felt that writing this book was particularly important, in light of the fact that so many organizations have undertaken reengineering without understanding what it is, what implications it presents for the organization and employees, and how to do it. A specific methodology, planned step-by-step in advance and yet flexible enough to accommodate new developments both within and outside the organization, is critical.

In this book we present our methodology. We don't pretend that it's fail-safe; nothing is. But it has worked for many organizations, leading to increased competitive advantage and instituting innovation as a way of life.

This second book in the *Warren Bennis Executive Briefing Series* makes use of the same SuperReading features that distinguished the first offering, *Fabled Service: Ordinary Acts, Extraordinary Outcomes.* Early feedback about these features, including pull quotes, bulleted lists of key points, highlighted facts, and crisp graphics, has been extremely positive, and we are gratified that we have been successful in easing the reader's task of learning about current business topics.

Warren Bennis
Santa Monica, CA, 1995

Authors' Preface

The 21st Century Organization: Reinventing Through Reengineering is not just another book about a trendy topic. This book is, first and foremost, a description of what actually happens when an enterprise is reinvented: what the critical success factors are, which organizational resources are brought to bear, how those resources are organized for a reengineering effort, what activities are completed—and how, by whom, and why. It is based on the methodology that we have developed and used to help organizations reengineer successfully.

From our point of view, this work offers certain advantages over other reengineering books:

- ◆ It's brief and concise. You can read it in very little time.
- ◆ It offers features designed to help you find information quickly and retain it more readily, for example, frequent headings, bullets, information showcased in shaded boxes, and "factoids" in the margin that augment the text.
- ◆ Its focus is extremely practical. You are spared any lengthy theoretical dissertations.
- ◆ It avoids the jargon often used in books on business or human resource development topics.
- ◆ Its tone is casual and, we believe, lively enough to keep you interested in our ideas.
- ◆ It includes cartoons and illustrations to lighten this serious, important topic.

In writing this book, we wanted to demystify the topic of reengineering, dispel some of the common myths about the topic, offer a brief but thorough treatment of our own methodology for conducting reengineering, and present the case for using this approach to competing in the 21st Century. If your organization decides to embark on reengineering—and we hope it does—we wish both you and the organization a successful journey.

We would like to express our gratitude to the many people who helped us complete this book. To our current and former business partners and colleagues, we say thanks for encouraging our efforts. Special thanks go to our clients, especially the fine people of Bausch & Lomb's Personal Products Division, who have the vision and courage to constantly move forward. To Dan Gill, Jim Kanaley, Charlie Hadeed, Jurij Kushner, Greg Nielsen, Bob Hribernik, Eugene Romeo,

Tom Moran, Bert Di Paola, Scott Rodgers, and Dave Pecora: Thanks for the support.

Several other authors and consultants have made pioneering and important contributions to the area of reengineering. In particular, to Michael Hammer, James Champy, Tom Davenport, James Brian Quinn, and Robert Tomasko, we would like to say thanks for the good work and for bringing the subject of reengineering to the forefront of management.

And this book never would have materialized without the tireless efforts of Do'reen Hein, Rhonda Kloosterman, Shirley Rodriguez, and the very professional staff of Pfeiffer & Company: Managing Editor JoAnn Padgett, who helped us plan our manuscript in the initial stages; Developmental Editor Carol Nolde, who edited the book with an emphasis on a succinct, orderly, and readable presentation; Production Editor Dawn Kilgore, who supervised the transformation of our manuscript into the beautiful work you have in your hands; and Senior Graphic Designer Lee Ann Hubbard, whose creative design, layout, and illustrations grace these pages. To everyone who spent countless hours with drafts, rewrites, and galleys, we express our heartfelt appreciation.

Finally, none of this would have been possible without the continuous inspiration, support, and confidence of our loving wives, Grace Gabe and Lynn Mische. We are so grateful that they are our partners in life.

Warren Bennis
Santa Monica, California

Michael A. Mische
Boalsburg, Pennsylvania

Foreword

Organizations are discovering that they cannot succeed in tomorrow's world unless they reinvent themselves today. Yet, despite this discovery, they often don't know what reinvention entails.

In *The 21st Century Organization: Reinventing Through Reengineering,* authors and consultants Warren Bennis and Michael A. Mische define what reengineering is and is not and then present their own five-phase methodology for performing reengineering. In essence, they have provided an effective road map for organizational transformation. Their book is an invaluable guide for any executive who is contemplating or initiating reengineering.

In giving us this book, Bennis and Mische also have encouraged what may well be the organization's most significant function: to serve as the enabler of what Edwin Land called "the rewarding and inspiring work day." In addition, this book fosters awareness of the organization as an entity through which the creativity of human minds continually raises people's living standard, thereby promoting the belief that tomorrow can be better than today.

It is my hope that courageous and innovative individuals like Bennis and Mische will be inspired by this book to address some of the important opportunities presented to organizations in the future:

- ♦ Generate a set of organizational titles that are more consistent with the leadership role than the outmoded management function. The title of "chief executive officer," for example, is an anachronism; "chief strategic officer" may be a possibility.

- ♦ Supplant the "chart" structure of the organization with a different structure that accommodates the interaction of a proactive culture with the reactive demands of influences outside the organization. The human nervous system with its simultaneous voluntary and involuntary capabilities may be an excellent model.

- ♦ Rethink out-of-date accounting systems, which make no allowance at all for the two most significant organizational assets: *knowledge* and *people.*

Donald Alstadt, Chairman of the Board, Lord Corporation

The term "reengineering," according to Ray Katz, writing in Quality Digest, was created to describe a creative and dynamic approach to business, but instead is being used as a euphemism for downsizing. And, says Katz, downsizing is neither creative nor dynamic. It's what business leaders do when they are out of ideas.[1]

WHAT IS REENGINEERING? MYTHS AND REALITIES

We started with a fresh sheet of paper and said to ourselves, "If we were starting GTE today, how would we do it?"

Bruce Carswell, GTE Corporation's
senior vice president of human resources

1

Today there's a growing tendency to charge headlong into an activity labeled "organizational reengineering." According to the media and organizational consultants, virtually all of the Fortune 500 companies are performing some type of reengineering. Even the U.S. government purportedly is attempting to reinvent itself.

Despite its popularity, the process of reengineering is still a mystery to many people. In an effort to help solve the mystery, we offer this chapter, in which we dispel some of the myths about reengineering, clarify the five essential elements of the process, present our detailed definition of reengineering, and describe the specific goals of reengineering. As you will see, the process of reengineering as we view and apply it is quite different not only from the applications of the past, but also from traditional problem-solving methods.

1

MYTHS ABOUT REENGINEERING

In working toward defining and describing a term that is so subject to controversy, we decided to start with some common misconceptions and describe what reengineering isn't:

Myth 1: If you're contemplating reengineering, you must have been doing all the wrong things, all along.

The reality is that if you've made it this far, you've done a number of things right, even if you haven't done them perfectly. The process of reengineering allows you to recognize successes while striving to identify and capitalize on opportunities for improvement through innovation.

Myth 2: Reengineering is about information technology.

The reality is that although information technology is an enabling agent of change and is essential to any reengineering effort, reinventing the enterprise requires a lot more than just addressing technology issues. History has shown that in and of itself, new technology never produces quantum results for shareholders and customers.

Myth 3: Reengineering means doing more with less.

The reality is that reengineering is about doing things differently and more effectively, with or without existing personnel. It does not start from the premise of eliminating jobs, nor does it inevitably lead to downsizing.

Downsizing does have its place in an organization that's overstaffed. The key point is that every job should create customer or shareholder value; if a job doesn't, it should be eliminated so that it doesn't simply contribute to growing overhead.

Unfortunately, during the downsizing movement of the 1990s some organizations went way too far, erroneously calling their efforts "reengineering," and cut deep into their core cultures. In doing so, they exorcised many of their values and leaders and lost not only knowledge, but also role models.

For those organizations that voluntarily forfeited their talent, downsizing became "suicisizing." They may have generated some short-term cost reductions and profits, but the overall cost to their long-term competitive posture has been enormous.

Myth 4: Reengineering can be used to fix any problem.

The reality is that reengineering is not a solution to be applied to isolated problems. It's a process that changes the organizational culture and creates new processes, new systems, new structures, and new ways to measure performance and success.

Myth 5: Reengineering can be managed by anyone.

The reality is that the person who serves as the transformation leader must have strong leadership skills, mature business judgment, extensive experience in managing organizational transformation, knowledge of the reengineering process, experience in using a refined methodology to conduct the process, and a

Technology-Driven Reengineering Gone Wrong

One Fortune 1000 company, a major distributor of brand-name and private-label products, invested about $7 million in new technology and software to support its order-entry and manufacturing processes. The stated goals of the effort were to enhance customer service, accelerate shipments, reduce head counts and inventories, and decrease cycle times.

Immediately after acquiring and installing the software, the company's consulting firm and information-services staff embarked on a multi-year, multi-million-dollar project to modify the new software. The objective was to enhance the software to better support "how we do business."

Despite the fact that the organization was heavily layered and rife with duplication of effort, no reengineering of the existing processes and organizational responsibilities was attempted. Senior management was convinced that it wasn't necessary and would only "disrupt the organization."

The new software was modified to support the processes that the company had used all along. Inventories, head counts, and cycle times were increased, not decreased. Customer service was not enhanced; shipments were not accelerated. The information-services staff was confronted with a backlog of user requests representing more than *thirty years* of effort and growing every day.

Downsizing Becomes "Suicisizing"

One major consulting firm used downsizing to cut its leadership group by some 25 percent. At the time of the downsizing, the firm was one of the leaders in its field.

Within three years of the initial downsizing, the firm went through at least four more reorganizations, all of which were significant. Business focus, morale, and core competencies deteriorated with each reorganization. Today this organization has dropped in comparative revenue rankings to virtually the bottom of its industry.

One way to judge if you are reengineering: The first time you bring it up, if no one screams, "Are you crazy?" then it is not a reengineering project.

Robert Rubin

commitment to helping the organization change. Credibility is a must.

Myth 6: Reengineering creates anxiety and chaos that are detrimental to the organization.

The reality is that reengineering does create anxiety, but anxiety need not be detrimental and chaos need not be the result. Reengineering is change, and change can be excruciatingly difficult. If the reengineering effort is properly managed and implemented, though, lasting scars can be avoided.

Myth 7: Reengineering is a scientific process.

The reality is that although certain scientific techniques might find their way into a reengineering process, the process itself is not a scientific one.

FIVE ESSENTIAL ELEMENTS OF REENGINEERING

Now that we've dispelled some of the myths commonly associated with reengineering, we can begin to build a new definition. In our view, reengineering has five essential elements:

♦ A bold vision.

♦ A systemic approach.

♦ A clear intent and mandate.

♦ A specific methodology.

♦ Effective and visible leadership.

Without any one of these five elements, the change effort being contemplated is not reengineering.

ESSENTIAL ELEMENT 1: A BOLD VISION

Some organizations that embark on efforts later called "reengineering" have been motivated by embarrassment, fear of extinction, or a wake-up call from competitors. (We offer some examples in Chapter 2 when we discuss the evolution of reengineering.) But a better motivation—the real starting point for successful reengineering—is a bold vision of the organization's future and the passion necessary to turn that vision into reality.

A few organizations, such as General Electric, Yamaha, Motorola, Kao, and Bausch & Lomb, have, in fact, reengineered out of vision and passion. All five of these companies were already doing well when the decision to reengineer was made.

Sometimes the necessary vision and passion arise from a desire to dominate or change an entire industry. Disney, for example, set out to regain dominance by reinventing its entertainment operations. It was driven by a passion not just to provide entertainment, but to *be* entertainment.

And Home Depot reengineered the way in which people shop for their home-remodeling

San Diego Historical Society, Photograph Collection

An old-fashioned hardware store, a good source of items for small jobs. Home Depot represents an alternative source concentrating on a wide range of services.

materials when it launched the concept of retail warehousing with huge quantities of in-stock items, everyday low prices, and highly paid and knowledgeable workers. In doing so it not only reengineered the traditional hardware and building-supply industries, but also created a completely new retailing concept.

ESSENTIAL ELEMENT 2: A SYSTEMIC APPROACH

Early in the evolution of reengineering, a number of organizations made change efforts that were *situational*, that is, specific to a particular problem. And therein lies the difference between what has been the historical context of reengineering and what we call "reengineering."

From our point of view, reengineering is *systemic*. It has far-reaching, organization-wide implications and is not restricted to just one organizational issue, procedure, task, activity, function, or unit.

Not everyone, however, shares our view. Reengineering definitions span a wide spectrum. At one end of the spectrum are the more traditional definitions, which characterize reengineering in a narrow context that emphasizes incremental improvement, changes to fundamental processes only, head-count reductions, and self-funding projects.

At the opposite end of the spectrum—where we happen to be—are the more revolutionary definitions, which characterize reengineering as total reinvention and transformation designed to achieve quantum results (minimum 50-percent improvement). The revolutionary view addresses all organizational functions in terms of the processes performed, whereas the traditional view confines itself to one or more individual activities within a specific function.

For example, let's assume that an organization is about to undergo reengineering. With the revolutionary approach, one of the functions dealt with would be customer service, and it would be addressed in its totality, just as all other functions within the organization would be. With the traditional approach, however, the effort might focus exclusively on a portion of customer service and, furthermore, only on one aspect of customer service, such as order entry.

The traditional approach doesn't lead to quantum results.

So what's wrong with the traditional approach? Customer service involves not just order entry, but various activities that are distributed throughout the average organization in various departments: credit, distribution, forecasting, sales, shipping, planning, scheduling, traffic, accounts receivable, and manufacturing. These activities are usually the responsibilities of different functional units, which treat and manage their components of customer service independently and differently from all other units.

Addressing the customer-service process using traditional, situational techniques might result in improvement to one or more activities of a specific procedure or department, but not to the process of customer service as a whole. In addition, not addressing other functions outside customer service—which may very well be related to customer service in ways that are not immediately apparent—might mean that benefits gained either will not be sustained or will be negated. Consequently, the customer may never see the results of the effort.

Always Remember Customers

Throughout the reengineering process, remember to ask John W. Nordstrom's favorite question: "What do our customers really want?"

Reengineering through reinventing, on the other hand, recognizes that the process of customer service spans many parts and levels of the typical organization, and it addresses all of those parts and levels. It arranges all activities associated with customer service—previously divided into separate units—into processes that have a continual flow, accelerated velocity, a consolidated function, and a common system of management practices and performance measurements. This organizational restructuring leads to uniformity in ways of dealing with customers and greatly increases the probability that customers will see the results of the reengineering effort.

There's another problem associated with the traditional approach: It doesn't lead to quantum results. Why? Because an effort intended to achieve incremental improvement is not designed to yield dramatic results; it is designed to satisfy an immediate need and reach a near-term objective.

ESSENTIAL ELEMENT 3: A CLEAR INTENT AND MANDATE

Thus far, very few organizations have embarked on reengineering with a clear intent and mandate. More often than not, an organization engages in some kind of change effort and after the fact refers to that effort as "reengineering" because that term has some internal appeal or external marketing value.

Instead, to effect systemic change that is lasting, the organization must start with that specific intention and must realize that the end point will be an entirely different enterprise. And creating a new enterprise requires the mandate and ongoing support of top management; there's no other way to ensure that the necessary resources are applied to plan, manage, implement, and sustain the reengineering effort.

ESSENTIAL ELEMENT 4: A SPECIFIC METHODOLOGY

Unlike the accounting and legal professions, reengineering has no codified rules, educational requirements, or professional standards. As reengineering is still evolving as a management doctrine, there is very little information on how to perform the process. In particular, there's an absence of "how-to" material described at a level that can be useful to a manager or executive.

But with a process as all-encompassing as reengineering, a specific methodology is critical. Both the leader of the reengineering process and the organizational employees who implement it need to know exactly what is to be done every step of the way. In the absence of specific techniques, the reengineering process can result in the chaos and lasting scars that we mentioned earlier when we were discussing reengineering myths.

ESSENTIAL ELEMENT 5: EFFECTIVE AND VISIBLE LEADERSHIP

Reengineering and the systemic transformation that results require effective and visible leadership. The leader of the process must have a number of skills and abilities:

♦ Creativity.

♦ Visionary influence.

♦ Solid knowledge of the business.

♦ Credibility achieved through a track record of successful experience in reengineering.

♦ Exceptional people skills, including the abilities to select the right people for implementing the reengineering effort and to provide positive and compelling coaching for them.

♦ Impeccable character.

♦ Excellent judgment.

UPI/Bettmann
Visionary leader and former U.S. Congress-woman Barbara Jordan

If the process leader does not have these skills and abilities, the reengineering effort will be compromised.

OUR DEFINITION OF "REENGINEERING"

Now that we've discussed what reengineering isn't and what it must have, we come to our definition:

> ***Reengineering is*** reinventing the enterprise by challenging its existing doctrines, practices, and activities and then innovatively redeploying its capital and human resources into cross-functional processes. This reinvention is intended to optimize the organization's competitive position, its value to shareholders, and its contribution to society.

Reinventing the enterprise is difficult. It means permanently transforming the entire orientation and direction of the organization. It means challenging and discarding traditional values, historical precedents, tried-and-true processes, and conventional wisdom and replacing them with entirely different concepts and practices. It means redirecting and retraining workers in accordance with those new concepts and practices.

The very cultural fiber of the enterprise must be interrogated and redefined. Traditional work flows must be examined and redesigned. Technology must be redirected from supporting individual users and departments to enabling new cross-functional processes and a flatter structure. New systems must be created to support personnel in making quick decisions that serve both the customer's and the organization's best interests. Ways of measuring and rewarding performance and success must be rethought.

What does this effort look like? We'll deal with the answer to this question in detail in subsequent chapters. For now, though, here's a sampling of the kinds of activities that characterize reengineering:

- ◆ Innovating.
- ◆ Listening to customers.
- ◆ Learning.
- ◆ Generating ideas.
- ◆ Designing new paradigms.

♦ Anticipating and eclipsing competitors.

♦ Contributing to the quality of the workplace and the community.

♦ Constructively challenging established management doctrines.

SPECIFIC GOALS OF REENGINEERING

Reengineering has five goals:

♦ Increasing productivity.

♦ Optimizing value to shareholders.

♦ Achieving quantum results.

♦ Consolidating functions.

♦ Eliminating unnecessary levels and work.

The following paragraphs explain these goals.

Goal 1: Increasing productivity. Reengineering seeks to increase productivity by creating innovative and seamless processes that have an uninterrupted flow and occur in a natural order, with a natural velocity.

The paradigm of vertical "silos" of tasks and responsibilities is broken down and replaced with a cross-functional, flatter, networked structure. The classical, top-down approach to control and decision making is replaced with an approach that is organized around core processes, is characterized by empowerment, and is closer to the customer.

Traditional organizational boundaries, which create gaps and "pass-offs" in work (and diminish the value, speed, and quality of processes), are eliminated. In Chapter 9 we discuss the implications of this change for employees.

Goal 2: Optimizing value to shareholders. Reengineering strives to optimize value to shareholders through doing things differently. Innovations in such functions as product

When Hallmark Cards created cross-functional teams of employees, those employees not only worked together but were in constant contact. Consequently, each employee was quickly aware of any changes that might affect his or her job. As a result, Hallmark reduced by 50 percent the time it took to develop certain lines of greeting cards.[2]

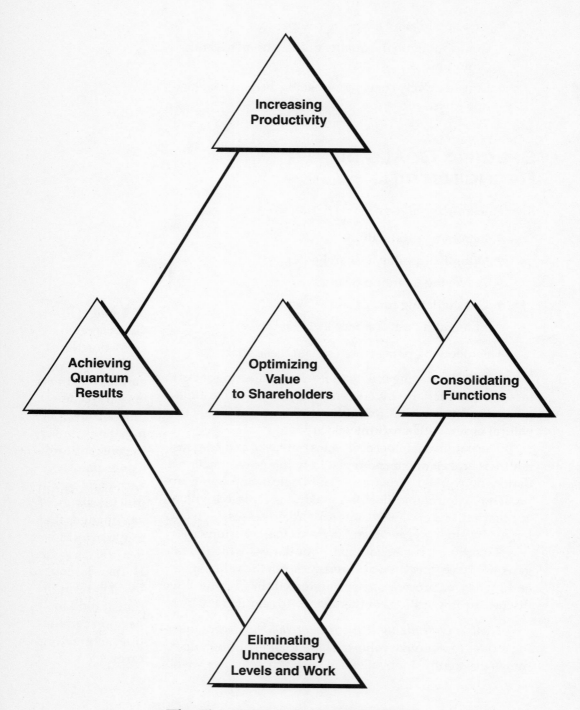

The Five Goals of Reengineering

design, manufacturing, and customer service are examples. Reengineering produces benefits for shareholders in these specific areas:

♦ Increased employee interest in and appreciation of the enterprise, its leadership, its products or services, and its customers.

♦ Improved internal cooperation, communication, teamwork, and understanding of needs.

♦ Increased employee knowledge of the organization's direction, its role in the marketplace, its competitors, and its identity.

♦ Improved matching of employee skills and empowerment to responsibilities and processes.

♦ New individual- and group-performance measures that are more closely aligned with the marketplace, the value of the work performed, and the contribution made.

Employees who are involved with reengineering recognize its benefits and develop a profound sense of ownership that helps the organization to achieve greater long-term growth and competitiveness.

Goal 3: Achieving quantum results. Reengineering sets out to achieve at least a 50-percent improvement; if the yield is not at least 50 percent, then the achievement, although it may be an impressive one, is not reengineering.

Our research and experience indicate the potential for these kinds of results:

♦ Productivity improvements of 25 to 100 percent.

♦ Head-count redeployments of 25 to 50 percent.

Quantum Results

When Chrysler began to reinvent itself, it looked long and hard at its processes and management practices and:

♦ Reduced its product-development-to-production time by 47 percent, thereby saving over a billion dollars.

♦ Shortened its product-delivery cycle by 46 percent.

♦ Implemented a revolutionary program with suppliers called SCORE, which saved over $400 million.

The results: 1993 was a record year for sales, earnings, and customer satisfaction.[3]

◆ Inventory reductions of 40 to 50 percent.

◆ Cycle-time improvements of 50 to 300 percent.

◆ Indirect-cost improvements of 25 to 50 percent.

These are not the traditional 5-, 10-, and 15-percent incremental-improvement gains that most organizations have been content to achieve.

Goal 4: Consolidating functions. Reengineering seeks to create an organization that is leaner, flatter, and faster. The ability to rapidly assimilate innovations, market needs, technological developments, customer trends, and competitor initiatives is a trademark of the reinvented organization.

Goal 5: Eliminating unnecessary levels and work. Reengineering constructively challenges and analyzes the organization's hierarchy and activities in terms of their value, purpose, and content. Organizational levels and activities that represent little value to shareholders or contribute little to competitiveness are either restructured or eliminated.

Reinvention requires the continual assessment of the organization, its management practices, its people, its systems, its customers, and the environment in which it operates. Five questions are asked, not once but repeatedly:

◆ Why does the organization do the things it does in the way it does them?

◆ What value is produced for customers and shareholders by performing this activity in this way?

◆ How could the organization perform this activity in a different way to enhance value?

◆ What innovative or breakthrough results does the organization want to achieve?

◆ What talents are required, and who within the organization has them?

Customer service representatives at CIGNA used to have to check with other departments such as billing to answer inquiries. A new system allowed them direct access to on-line information. The result? A productivity improvement of 35 percent and a cost reduction of 65 percent for CIGNA.[4]

Conclusion

Reengineering transforms an organization from what it is now into an unlimited universe of what it could be. Reengineering is not a fad; it is a distinct and permanent change in how an organization can be led, managed, and operated and how its performance can be measured.

Even though we've clarified what reengineering is, there are still a number of unanswered questions:

◆ How is reengineering done?

◆ Is there a good methodology for performing reengineering?

◆ If so, who carries out that methodology?

◆ What pitfalls commonly plague reengineering efforts?

◆ What are the most significant determinants of success?

◆ Are there guidelines on how to succeed?

◆ What is the impact of reengineering on the organization?

◆ What types of teams and people are needed to do reengineering?

The remaining chapters offer our answers to these questions.

What makes an "adaptive" organizational culture? John Kotter and James Heskett, authors of Corporate Culture and Performance, say that it's managers who listen to customers and value employees. These managerial characteristics enable organizations to adapt to external economic forces very quickly. Kotter and Heskett found that in almost all cases they examined, adaptive organizations outperformed nonadaptive organizations in terms of net income growth, return on investment, and increased stock price.[1]

Why Reengineer? The Need for Change

The one thing that frightens senior management and other key personnel more than any other factor is the unknown.

Bill Wyllie, specialist in "corporate resurrection"

2

Many people have an image of the annual meetings of organizations as sedate social gatherings where the auditor's year-end report is a topic of civil discussion. This image probably was accurate at one time, but no longer.

In today's world, annual meetings, like political elections, are often tumultuous affairs. Shareholders, like taxpayers, are demanding higher standards of performance, more effective management, greater accountability, and enhanced value from their leaders.

Those who have a stake in the ability of the private sector to deliver earnings and the ability of the public sector to pro-

duce cost-effective services are no longer satisfied with learning what happened last year or why something didn't work the way it was supposed to. They want to know about tomorrow, and they're demanding an effective way to get there.

TRADITIONAL METHODS YIELD UNIMPRESSIVE RESULTS

Hardly a day goes by without comments from business or public-sector leaders on why their organizations need to be leaner and faster in the competitive arena of "the new world order." It's no wonder that leaders now speak in terms of being the lowest-cost and highest-quality providers of products or services. Certainly this goal is laudable in an era that places a premium on value and world-class performance.

But is this goal achievable by using traditional management practices?

> *The results from the practices of the last twenty years are in, and they are not impressive.*

Despite the hiring of masses of MBAs, huge investments in information technology, mandatory attendance at management seminars, and the adoption of a litany of short-term and quick-fix management trends, most organizations are not significantly better or more competitive for their efforts.

In fact, overall performance and results have been disappointing, if not outright dismal. Why is it that even historically stalwart companies are now scrambling to find new life?

Unless you learn to manage the aftereffects of winning, the forces that led your team to the top will turn around and destroy you.

Pat Riley

LOOKING FOR THE ANSWER

Typical answers, which revolve around the economy, quality, and productivity, have fallen short of explaining why organizations are not becoming more competitive.

It's not the swings in the economy, although they certainly influence everyone.

And it's not quality issues. Quality affects preferences, but quality, for the most part, has been improving. In fact, the large gap in quality that at one time existed between U.S. products and those produced in Japan and Germany—especially in the automotive, fabricated-steel, and consumer-electronics industries—has narrowed and in some cases is indiscernible.

It's not lost productivity, either. The emerging economies of Korea, China, and their Pacific Rim neighbors, along with those of Mexico and Latin America, are currently considered low-cost labor markets that artificially distort the value of human capital in more advanced economies and, consequently, make products that are more price competitive. However, the companies that maintain operations in these nations also run profitable operations in the advanced economies.

Another factor related to productivity is sometimes cited as a suppressor of U.S. growth, sales, and profitability: organized labor or the lack of worker involvement. However, as there is no shortage of products to sell, obviously the U.S. does employ skilled labor effectively.

So if it's none of these elements—not the economy, nor quality, nor productivity—that accounts for poor performance, what does account for it? To answer this question, we need to review the historical development of various models for managing an enterprise.

Economist **Juliet B. Schor, who examined past and present work habits of U.S. workers, concluded that the average worker is twice as productive now as in 1948.**[2]

THE HISTORY OF MANAGEMENT

STOCK MONTAGE

Abraham Maslow, noted psychologist whose ideas revolutionized management

The management practices in the majority of organizations today are the product of several centuries of economic expansion, free-market evolution, and industrial engineering. All of these practices have evolved from concepts first proposed by such management luminaries as Frederic Taylor, Alfred Sloan, Henry Ford, Luther Gulick, Douglas McGregor, and Abraham Maslow.

The socioeconomic context of the period in which these concepts and models were developed—the 18th and late 19th Centuries and the industrial-expansion years of the 20th Century—provided for a relatively orderly and predictable environment characterized by:

♦ High market growth.

♦ Continued economic expansion.

♦ Strong nationalism.

♦ Massive migration of European cultures to the U.S.

♦ The standardization of products and manufacturing techniques.

♦ Increasing personal income.

♦ Simplification of work to its smallest elements.

♦ Homogeneous markets.

♦ Strict chains of managerial control.

♦ The vertical integration of the enterprise.

In the era following World War II, being competitive meant concentrating on gaining efficiencies and economies of scale through repetitive work, task simplification, mass production, and high volumes. In other words, bigger was better.

> *Most operational processes are transaction driven: Do more of the same, but do it faster and with greater control.*

Many organizations believed that getting closer to the customer required opening new field offices, adding warehouses, conducting more focus groups, and having legions of salespeople traveling all over the planet. Strategic and organizational planning was defined as last year's results plus 20 percent and was organized around strict financial goals and head counts.

Although seasonal factors were taken into account, cycle times for concepts, products, and markets were essentially driven by and for the convenience of the organization, not its customers.

TRANSACTION-DRIVEN ORGANIZATIONS

The post-World War II management mentality just described is perpetuated in many, if not most, U.S. organizations today. As a result, most operational processes are transaction driven: Do more of the same, but do it faster and with greater control.

In most organizations, each transaction has its own responsible person and department as well as unique work methods and ways to measure performance. Each transaction is designed around certain assumptions, standards, and strict accounting and management controls that create an enormous number of exceptions. The exceptions necessitate special rules for handling, which then drive the need for more standards, more procedures,

The Bettmann Archive
Factory workers in the 1940s

more controls, and more personnel—all of which require more organizational layers.

Somehow, the voice of the customer usually gets lost. When it is heard, it is ignored, diluted by the organization, or misinterpreted. Service and the trading relationship thus become secondary; the perpetuation of the organization's model is primary.

TRENDY MANAGEMENT APPROACHES

Confronted with increasingly greater pressures to perform, many organizations in the 1980s and 1990s turned to trendy management approaches such as total quality management (TQM), activity value assessment, continuous quality improvement (CQI), and self-managed work teams (SMT).

Although many of these approaches produced direct results in the form of incremental or function-specific improvements, most failed to produce any significant breakthrough, competitive advantage, or direct financial returns. Instead, organizations faced the unpleasant reality that they were no better off.

The Disappointment of Trendy Approaches

According to a study prepared by the Electric Power Research Institute, satisfaction with trendy approaches ranges from only 35 percent to 60 percent among executives who attempted to implement such programs. A similar study performed by the consulting firm of Sibson & Co. produced even more dismal results: Satisfaction ranged from a high of 40 percent to a low of 10 percent.

WHAT TODAY'S REALITY MEANS

Today's reality proves that what traditionally worked does not work anymore; neither do trendy methods. The growth of U.S. domestic markets has slowed and in many segments has actually declined. Debt and deficits continue to haunt individuals, governments, and businesses and inhibit capital formation and private investment.

Both the quantity and caliber of competition have increased. Technology has given rise to instantaneous information flows and transactions.

Along with these changes has come a change in individual and societal demands.

> *Whereas people were formerly concerned with issues involving price and quantity, now they are primarily concerned with value and service.*

This new reality is not transitory. It is a systemic and permanent change in society and the business world.

PREDICTIONS ABOUT THE NEW REALITY

To help define the competitive arena of the mid-1990s and the 21st Century, we offer the following observations about twelve trends that will characterize this period:

Trend 1: Global markets will become saturated. The marketplace will be glutted with products, services, and suppliers. A given product can no longer be expected to dominate, as there will be price and quality parity among products as well as universal accessibility to products. Any strategic advantage gained through a product will be temporary, because that product will be copied quickly and easily.

Trend 2: Technological advantages will be short-lived. Information technology will be replicated quickly; thus, any

DILBERT® by Scott Adams

DILBERT® reprinted by permission of UFS, Inc.

From 1945 to 1980, many single-income households in the U.S. enjoyed a solid, middle-class existence. Housing costs and automobile expenses represented only 25 percent and a maximum of 10 percent, respectively, of monthly income.

In the 1990s, U.S. housing usually requires more than 30 percent of a monthly income for a dual-income family, with new-car prices approaching another 20 to 25 percent. Instead of trading the old car for a new one every three years, as they did formerly, people in the U.S. either keep a car for seven or eight years or lease one.

significant competitive advantage obtained through technology will be quickly neutralized. Information technology will enable the work force to be spread out globally, even though the enterprise is consolidated or headquartered at a specific location.

Trend 3: Service will be critical. As consumers become more knowledgeable, better educated, and more discriminating, markets will become more competitive. Consumers will mandate the level of quality, establish prices, and define and set the value for products or services. Quality and good price will be essential but expected. The service and the experience that the consumer has in the relationship with the service provider will be the differentiating factors.

Trend 4: Growth in disposable incomes will slow. The markets for consumer products and durable goods will become tighter and more competitive as the growth rate in disposable income and savings continues to slow. Conversely, consumer debt and taxes as a percentage of aggregate household income will increase. Thus, the velocity of spending will stabilize, creating a more intensive competitive marketplace characterized by a decline in mass markets and a proliferation of micro-markets and customized mass production.

Trend 5: Income gaps will widen. Consumer and government debt and deficits will compromise the abilities of both individuals and governments to create wealth and increase capital formation, especially in the U.S., Canada, and a number of European nations. As a result, the rate of increase in the general standard of living will be slower than that of the period from 1945 to 1990. The gap between those who live well and those of the middle- and lower-income groups will widen, and higher-income consumers will become more discriminating.

Trend 6: Europe will achieve economic unification. Europe will unite economically under a single currency or trading medium. Although nationalism may prevent any meaningful political unification, at least in the near term of the 21st Century, economic consolidation is inevitable.

Service and the ability to assimilate change rapidly will be the most important components of success in the 21st Century.

Trend 7: The Pacific Rim will hold the greatest potential for growth. The greatest growth markets and potential for employment reside in the Pacific Rim. The nations that compose this area have industrious cultures, growing economies, and evolving infrastructures capable of supporting the global deployment of resources and organizational capabilities, the creation of personal wealth, and high growth rates in personal income and consumption.

Trend 8: Technology will be the great equalizer. Service and the ability to assimilate change rapidly will be the most important components of success in the 21st Century.

To be competitive, an organization will have to be technology enabled. And its people will use that technology not just to perform transactions but also to analyze information to support the decision-making process. Applications and data will be accessible, scalable to needs, and uniformly defined.

The specific types of technology and vendors will be unimportant, as most organizations will either have access to or actually have similar technology. However, how the organization deploys its technological assets and resources to achieve differentiation will make the difference in whether it is competitive.

Trend 9: The work force will be transitory. Employment practices in many developed and advanced nations, such as the U.S., Japan, the U.K., Germany, and Italy, are changing from lifetime careers to transitory arrangements with contract personnel. Organizations will have a smaller percentage of full-time employees with core competencies and a larger percentage of highly specialized contract workers.

A skilled worker will probably have multiple employers, a portfolio of jobs, and a variable income. A worker's

In the heyday of the industrial era, a young professional with a college degree could expect to average no more than three company changes during a forty-year career. Today's sociologists and business psychologists predict at least six to eight job changes for a new college graduate.

worth and compensation in the marketplace will not be measured by the traditional concepts of title and time spent in a job, but rather by skills, diversity of experience, and the financial return of the job portfolio.

Trend 10: Social enclaves will emerge in the U.S. There will be a permanent migration of professionals and skilled workers away from urban areas to lower-density areas and social enclaves. This movement has already begun and is being precipitated by a number of socioeconomic and technological influences:

- ♦ The continuing degradation of urban lifestyles.
- ♦ Crime.
- ♦ The cost of living.
- ♦ The creation of the job portfolio (see Trend 9).
- ♦ Information technology, which has enabled an individual to telecommute and transact business from virtually anywhere.

Technology and communications are making both the work force and consumers highly mobile, independent of traditional support structures, extremely competent, and very productive.

Trend 11: Economic boundaries will be transparent. As organizations strive to cultivate new and existing customers in increasingly competitive markets, provide service to those customers, optimize manufacturing and supplier resources, identify emerging opportunities, and prioritize investments, geographical demarcations will be essentially nonexistent.

Trend 12: Breakthrough performance will only be achieved by making use of intellectual assets. There's no other way to generate the kind of performance that will carry an organization to success in the new reality.

THE ANSWER: REINVENTING THE ORGANIZATION

It seems clear that the new reality will involve profound transformation. And herein lies the problem. Many organizations are simply not equipped to assimilate and respond to rapid changes in the market, technology, competition, and customer and constituent needs. Instead, they are structured and managed according to leadership and organizational models that were developed long ago and for a different world order. To flourish and sustain itself in the 21st Century, today's organization must reinvent itself to create the enterprise of tomorrow.

It makes little difference whether the organization is for profit, not for profit, or a government agency. That enterprise must be leaner, faster, and smarter—able to change quickly along with the other elements of its environment.

To flourish and sustain itself in the 21st Century, today's organization must reinvent itself to create the enterprise of tomorrow.

THE EVOLUTION OF REINVENTION THROUGH REENGINEERING

For those few organizations that have taken the first steps into the realm of reengineering and have been successful, the results have been nothing short of remarkable. Organizations such as Yamaha, Harley-Davidson, Toyota, Matsushita, Pepsico, BMW, Disney, Merck, Baxter, and AT&T are in a

An Interesting Observation

"People don't come to work here because they want to be challenged. They come here to do their jobs and make their mortgage payments. They aren't interested in innovating or making changes, and we aren't in the business of entertaining hot-shot MBAs."

So said one company's vice president of human resources during a brief but memorable exit interview with one of the authors. An anecdote? Perhaps. But the kind of thinking it represents is symptomatic of the many problems that organizations face today.

Yamaha reinvented the market for pianos by creating additional value for customers— not by reinventing an already great product, but by enhancing the ownership experience. Yamaha married the leading technology of the compact-disc player with the beloved player piano. The resulting product was offered at less than half the cost of a piano.

constant state of evolution. They are continually reinventing themselves and, as a result, are held in high regard by the competition, customers, and stakeholders.

For example, a major insurance company reduced claim-processing time by 85 percent. Motorola reduced direct and indirect operating costs by $1 billion over a four-year period. A manufacturer of consumer goods cut its product-development time by 60 percent. Another manufacturer was able to reduce its customer-order cycle time by 60 percent while improving its service and lowering its transaction costs by more than 25 percent and its inventories by 14 percent.

CHRYSLER'S SUCCESS

The examples just cited are certainly compelling, particularly from a financial perspective. However, reinventing the organization is more than process change. Perhaps one of the best examples of early reengineering—indeed, resurrection—is the process undergone at Chrysler Corporation.

Chrysler came to understand that a number of factors were important in the successful management of automobile manufacturing—not only quality and price, but also product design, ergonomics, and the way a product is presented in the marketplace. In the late 1980s when Chrysler began to falter for the second time in a decade, its leadership recognized that reinventing itself and the way it visualized, designed, produced, and presented cars to the consumer were essential to its long-term survival.

The company began to use cross-functional teams that involved accounting, sales, marketing, engineering, parts, and manufacturing in the design of what ultimately has become the LH car. With its cab-forward design and its integrated engineering concepts, the Chrysler LH car literally swept the sales sweepstakes in the North American automotive market. This innovative design, which now

The Chrysler LH

includes Concorde, Intrepid, Vision, and Cirrus, is an extremely powerful testament to organizational reinvention thorough reengineering.

FORD'S EXPERIENCE

Another much-heralded example of early reengineering is that of Ford Motor Company.

> *Ford, which had more than five hundred administrative personnel assigned to its accounts-payable function, learned that Mazda accomplished the same function with only five people.*

Ford conducted an analysis and concluded that its accounts-payable and receipt-of-goods procedures not only were too complex, but also involved duplication of effort. Its long-standing management practices contributed to the complexity and to work fragmentation. Exceptions became the rules, which required additional people, and vendors were free to send Ford anything at any time.

Obviously the accounts-payable function was ripe for improvement efforts, and Ford subsequently reengineered this function. Ford was successful in its reengineering effort, but this story also points out an important issue: How did the leadership of a publicly held corporation ever allow an overhead function to expand to more than five hundred people? If a single overhead function in any organization requires that many people, reengineering can be accomplished readily and should easily yield dramatic results.

HARLEY-DAVIDSON'S RESURGENCE

A reinvention of wider scope was accomplished by Harley-Davidson, which roared back from the brink of bankruptcy not once, but twice. In the process of its transformation, Harley-Davidson recognized that there was a direct linkage

Harley-Davidson completely redesigned its image in the global marketplace.

between its customers, the motorcycles it made, its dealer network, and its manufacturing process. Using this understanding, Harley-Davidson set about reinventing not only the company, but also the very experience of owning a motorcycle.

The astonishing results of the Harley-Davidson reinvention process are documented in Peter Reid's book *Well Made in America: Lessons from Harley-Davidson on Being the Best.* When the company began reinventing itself, the Japanese and German motorcycle manufacturers had already displaced it from its number-one market-share position in large motorcycles in North America; at that time Harley-Davidson's market share had fallen to a dismal 12 percent.

In the course of reinventing itself and focusing on the customer, Harley-Davidson completely redesigned its distribution network, its dealer relationships, its supplier network, the quality of its accessory products, and—most important—its image in the global marketplace. Today the company owns more than 65 percent of the market for large motorcycles in North America. Better still, every motorcycle that Harley-Davidson builds is sold in advance, and the waiting list for its products spans months at a time.

Like Chrysler, Harley-Davidson was facing incredible competitive pressures, long odds of success, and imminent demise. Like Chrysler, it experienced a profound need for change. Both companies recognized their needs and benefited from strong leadership that challenged the traditional doc-

©1987 by FORBES Inc. Courtesy of the FORBES Archives. Photo by: Glen A. Davis

Malcolm Forbes, prominent businessman and Harley-Davidson enthusiast

trine and power structures. Both formed cross-functional teams that combined efforts in a synergistic fashion to ensure world-class results. For each of these companies, the effort of reinvention addressed not just fundamental business practices, but the very fiber of the organization.

CONCLUSION

Organizations like Chrysler, Ford, and Harley-Davidson were pioneers. Although the process of reengineering has evolved today into something quite different from what they did, these early practitioners of reengineering took the first bold steps in an activity that subsequently inspired other organizations to replicate and enlarge on their efforts.

These pioneers saw that they were faced with massive environmental changes, necessitating massive internal changes in response. For them, reengineering became the road not just to success, but to survival.

It has since become clear that no organization is immune from change, the advance of civilization, and the will of the marketplace. To survive and grow in the 21st Century, all organizations must reinvent themselves.

John Farrell, *writing in* Planning Review, *notes that companies that have a better chance for success in reengineering share many of the same characteristics:*

♦ *They operate in constantly changing customer, competitive, and product/service environments.*

♦ *They have balanced perspectives between long-term strategic gains and short-term results.*

♦ *They can quickly develop and implement major new or changed organizations, technologies, and systems.*

♦ *They view business processes and organizational structures as enhancers of successful performance.*

♦ *They have a management and employee culture accountable for increasing levels of performance.*[1]

Avoiding Failure: A Methodology for Success

The will to win is important, but the will to prepare is vital.

Joe Paterno, coach of the
Pennsylvania State University
Nittany Lions

3

In this chapter we present our methodology for reengineering, one that has worked many times for us. But we also want to caution you that, regrettably, there is no fail-safe approach. Reinventing an organization that has enjoyed success and has a deeply rooted culture is not a trivial undertaking.

Long-standing beliefs, doctrines, and ways of doing things must be constructively challenged and organizational barriers and cultural bias overcome. The historical definitions of success and traditional methods for career progression and management practices must be evaluated, redefined, and recast. The reengineering process must unite many divergent interests, needs, skills, and departments into highly effective, cross-functional, and integrated business units.

It's no wonder that, with a process of this scope, approximately 70 to 80 percent of all reengineering efforts end in failure—failure in the sense that the effort did not produce the intended results or that the experience was extremely negative. Consequently, in this chapter we also address the major pitfalls of reengineering and the warning signs associated with each.

In our zeal to caution you against possible pitfalls and in stating the high failure rate of reengineering efforts, we don't want to mislead you into thinking that reengineering isn't worth the effort or the risk. On the contrary, this revolutionary approach, done correctly, will do more for an organization than anything it has tried thus far. Remember that the 20 to 30 percent of organizations that succeed at reengineering are positioning themselves for greatness in the coming century.

Pitfalls to Avoid

There are, of course, many reasons that a reengineering effort might fail, but the most prevalent reason is misunderstanding, as shown in the following eight major pitfalls. We offer this information in the belief that watching for and reacting to the warning signs of each pitfall will help to protect your organization against failure.

Pitfall 1: Inappropriate use. Sometimes organizations fail at reengineering because they are not reinventing themselves. Instead of seeking systemic change and process innovation, they attempt to apply reengineering to fix specific problems. In these situational cases, the organization is almost always using the latest reengineering jargon while perpetuating traditional methods, structures, and practices.

Here are the warning signs that an organization is headed for an inappropriate use of reengineering:

♦ Applying reengineering too broadly or attempting to use reengineering as a cure for chronic leadership and management problems.

♦ Selectively trying to use reengineering without making the corresponding organizational changes.

♦ Being myopic about processes, people, and the challenges involved.

♦ Being overconfident and attempting too many reengineering projects.

Pitfall 2: Lack of vision. As we discussed in Chapter 1, having a clear vision for the organization is essential for any reengineering effort. Reinvention does not occur by chance or destiny. It is the result of hard work and a defined course of action.

These are the warning signs that an organization may lack a vision:

♦ Being unable to produce a clear vision statement or definitive objectives.

♦ Focusing on specific departments rather than on cross-functional tasks.

♦ Restricting the reengineering effort to the practices that take place within traditional organizational boundaries.

Pitfall 3: Ineffective reengineering team(s). Reengineering occurs as the result of human effort. Therefore, it is essential that the project be led and staffed by a team (or teams) whose members are skilled and effective. However, most internal resources do not have the tools, experience, and perspective to reinvent effectively, and very few are afforded the time necessary to commit to the process.

The following are warning signs that an organization has or is creating an ineffective team:

♦ Assigning inappropriate resources to the effort.

♦ Failing to create a team that is committed full-time to the effort.

♦ Failing to assign dedicated working space to the team.

♦ Failing to designate sponsorship and "protection" for the team.

♦ Organizing the team as a traditional project team.

♦ Failing to adjust measurements of compensation and success to reflect participation on the team.

Pitfall 4: Inappropriate empowerment. Empowerment is an elusive and delicate matter. In reengineering, employee empowerment is necessary to challenge the status quo and to design and implement change. However, the degree of empowerment is important; either too much or too little can lead to failure.

The warning signs of an inappropriate degree of empowerment are these:

♦ Providing so much empowerment that leadership and management are diluted.

♦ Providing so little empowerment that traditional doctrines are not challenged.

♦ Providing "phantom" empowerment that's here today, gone tomorrow.

Pitfall 5: Rationalization of process. Often reengineering is embraced by the organization's leaders until it affects their areas. When threatened in this way, managers sometimes react by rationalizing why a process should be reengi-

Defining "Empowerment"

Empowerment means removing bureaucratic boundaries that box people in and keep them from making the most effective use of all of their skills, experiences, energies, and ambitions. It means allowing them to develop a sense of ownership over parts of the process that are uniquely their responsibility, while at the same time demanding that they accept a share of the broader responsibility and ownership of the whole process.[2]

neered, so that the activities, turf, and people in their areas are protected. Thus, the organization will appear to have done much work, but in actuality few changes are made.

Here are the warning signs of rationalization:

♦ Forcing processes and work flows to match the design of the existing organization.

♦ Seeking ways to justify the status quo.

♦ Achieving only incremental improvements.

♦ Avoiding the elimination of processes and people.

♦ Preserving traditional structures and tasks.

Pitfall 6: Relying exclusively on information technology. It may seem that we're unable to let go of this issue, but the fact is that relying on technology alone is what many organizations call reengineering—and it does not transform the enterprise.

The warning signs of relying on information technology are as follows:

♦ Automating how things are done today (as opposed to automating reengineered processes or activities).

♦ Accelerating existing process flows.

♦ Automating the obvious.

♦ Buying the latest and greatest technology.

Pitfall 7: Use of geographical and organizational boundaries to demarcate differences. Assembling autonomous operating units was an effective way to get work done in the past. Read an emphasis on the last phrase in that sentence—*in the past.* The global enterprise of today and tomorrow requires a different structure and a different set of management practices.

Reengineering views all locations and operating units as parts of a single entity, identifies common needs and measures of performance and success, recognizes unique requirements, and neutralizes any anomalies. The resulting consistency in strategies, operating principles, processes, and technologies supports a leaner, faster, more intelligent, and more competitive organization.

These are the warning signs that an organization may be striving to create or keep boundaries that would lead to reengineering failure:

♦ Viewing distributed, decentralized, or geographically remote locations as different, separate, or unique.

♦ Entirely avoiding autonomous operations.

Pitfall 8: Failure to understand the reengineering process and its implications. Reengineering is difficult! It requires stamina, commitment, and adherence to a responsive methodology. Expectations are often overstated, while the effort and implications of the journey are underestimated. Those involved in reengineering need to have a profound respect for its scope and complexity.

The following are warning signs that people may not understand what's involved in reengineering:

♦ Being unable to discuss the phases and implications of the reengineering process.

♦ Selectively using reengineering to avoid or reinforce politics.

♦ Viewing the effort dispassionately.

How to Succeed

Now that we've presented the bad news, let's proceed to the good news: There are, in fact, ways to ease the reengineering journey and put your organization on the road to success. The three most significant determinants of whether a reengineering effort succeeds or fails are these:

♦ Creating a bold and sweeping vision.

♦ Having access to, understanding, and using an appropriate methodology for reengineering.

♦ Staffing the reengineering team(s) appropriately.

In the following paragraphs we outline our five-phase methodology for reengineering and present guidelines for success. Then in Chapters 4 through 8 we discuss each phase in detail. In Chapter 9 we discuss the human element of reengineering, including staffing issues.

OUR MODEL FOR REENGINEERING

Reengineering cannot be approached in an unstructured and informal manner. Reinventing the enterprise necessitates a responsive, comprehensive, and effective methodology developed specifically for creating process innovation and lasting organizational transformation.

Our reengineering model has been carefully crafted to allow application in a variety of organizations regardless of size; orientation as a profit, not-for-profit, or governmental entity; or industry. Using our methodology will also help to avoid the pitfalls that we just discussed.

It's important to stress that no methodology can address every situation that might arise during the complex process of reengineering. The application of any methodology is unique to the specific organization involved. Nevertheless, having a template to follow is critical.

The Five Phases of the Model

Our model, which is illustrated on the following page, is organized into five phases:

♦ Phase 1: Visioning and Setting Goals.

♦ Phase 2: Benchmarking and Defining Success.

♦ Phase 3: Innovating Processes.

♦ Phase 4: Transforming the Organization.

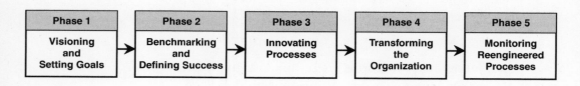

Phase 1	Phase 2	Phase 3	Phase 4	Phase 5
Visioning and Setting Goals	Benchmarking and Defining Success	Innovating Processes	Transforming the Organization	Monitoring Reengineered Processes

The Five Phases of Reengineering

♦ Phase 5: Monitoring Reengineered Processes.

Each phase has its own distinct objectives, targets, tasks, and resulting products. Because the reengineering process must reflect the specific needs of the organization, there are no time limits for performing each phase. The unique needs of the organization involved will dictate the level of complexity, precise work steps, and schedule for the reengineering project.

Within each phase are what we call *process clusters,* each of which is a combination of work steps, individual tasks, work products, and formal deliverables. Each work step can be expanded, eliminated, or tailored to address the unique requirements of the organization and the overall reengineering project. As illustrated on the next page, there are twenty-one process clusters in the entire model.

If you want to be the greatest company, you have to start acting like one today.

Tom Watson, Sr.

Timing in Using the Model

Our general rule is that reengineering should produce measurable results within a period of twelve to fifteen months. An effort that exceeds fifteen months is susceptible to failure,

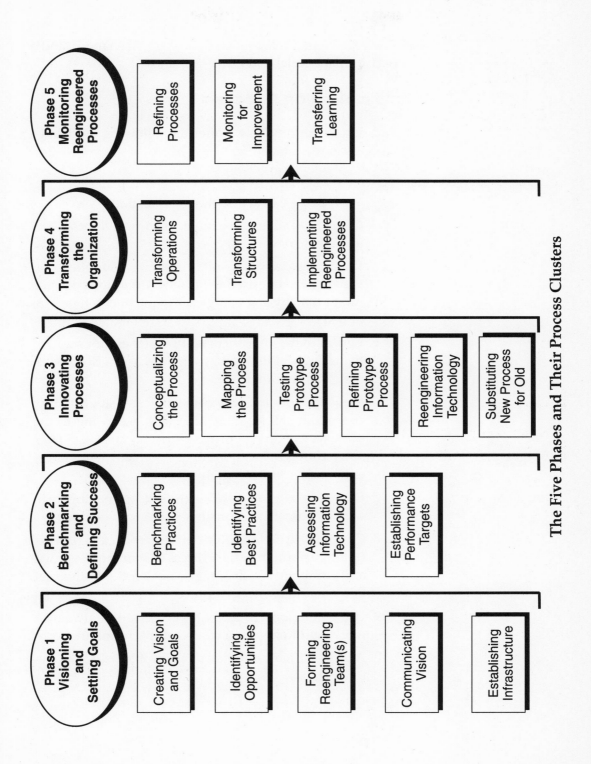

The Five Phases and Their Process Clusters

because it is vulnerable to inertia, directional changes, and a variety of managerial and other influences.

GUIDELINES FOR SUCCESS

In addition to our model, we offer the following guidelines for success in reengineering:

1. Think broadly, boldly, and openly.
2. View processes across the organization.
3. Challenge all traditional doctrines and processes and create new ones.
4. Determine desired results. Organize your efforts by viewing each desired result as a continuous process rather than by analyzing each department, function, or task.
5. Link activities in concurrent processes, not sequential tasks. Make sure that activities are performed in their natural order.
6. View each organizational location as a single entity; consolidate all locations logically, according to the same way of doing business. (Just because resources are in different locations does not make them different or subject to exceptions.)
7. Empower employees to make decisions having to do with customers and processes that they deal with.
8. Concentrate on the value derived from each process (the contribution of the process to shareholder value and competitive advantage), not on the individual tasks that make up that process.
9. Use technology to enable a process, to harmonize work, and to improve value and performance.
10. Act on difficult decisions and problems. Make the tough calls.

11. Create cross-functional teams composed of people from appropriate levels and having appropriate skills. Use external resources such as consultants.

12. Be realistic about the magnitude of the effort. Reengineering is difficult, radical, and significant.

CONCLUSION

While it's true that there are a number of pitfalls that an enterprise call fall into, there are also a number of ways to increase an organization's chances for success. Being prepared, staying vigilant, and using a solid methodology are three of the keys.

As you read through the next five chapters covering the five phases of our model, try envisioning your own organization as it undergoes a reengineering effort: What would you do if you were to reinvent the enterprise today?

As leadership researchers and experts James M. Kouzes and Barry Z. Posner suggest, there is no freeway to the future—often not even paved roads, but instead uncertain terrain and wilderness. So pioneering leaders rely on a compass and a dream. They look to the future with a sense of what is uniquely possible, and they passionately believe that people working together can make a difference. Visions are the leader's magnetic north; they give direction and purpose to the organization.[1]

PHASE 1: VISIONING AND SETTING GOALS

We are not just planning for the future; we are inventing it.

Thomas W. Sidlik, CEO of
Chrysler Financial Corporation

4

The starting point for any reengineering effort is the creation of a vision. The vision, as we mentioned earlier, must:

♦ Be sweeping and bold, stressing quantum rather than incremental results.

♦ Create a sense of energy, passion, and commitment rather than anxiety, panic, and intimidation.

♦ Be realistic and achievable, serving as a guide for all organizational activity.

Once the vision has been created, near- and long-term goals must be devised to turn the vision into reality.

PHASE 1 PROCESS CLUSTERS

Phase 1 includes five process clusters:

Wayne Gretzky, who became the National Hockey League's all-time leading scorer at age twenty-eight, was once asked what made him a great hockey player. He was exceptional, he answered, "because I go where the puck is going to be, not where it is." [2]

45

Objectives of Phase 1

♦ **Create and communicate the vision for the reinvented enterprise.**

♦ **Establish and launch the reengineering effort.**

♦ **Develop the appropriate goals and measures of performance and success for the reengineering effort.**

♦ **Establish and communicate expectations.**

♦ **Coordinate resources and form the reengineering team(s) that will carry out the effort.**

♦ 1.1: Creating a Vision and Goals.

♦ 1.2: Identifying Opportunities.

♦ 1.3: Forming and Educating the Reengineering Team(s).

♦ 1.4: Communicating the Vision and Gaining Commitment.

♦ 1.5: Establishing an Infrastructure.

In the following paragraphs you'll find an explanation of each of these clusters.

PROCESS CLUSTER 1.1: CREATING A VISION AND GOALS

The initial process cluster of the reengineering journey is one of the most important activities involved: creating a clear statement about what the enterprise wants to be and where it wants to go. Creating the vision involves a number of activities:

♦ Ascertaining competitor capabilities and actions.

♦ Identifying environmental drivers and influences.

♦ Assessing the organization's needs, constraints, and capabilities.

♦ Linking the organization's desired direction to tangible business needs, goals, and plans.

♦ Deciding whether or not to adopt a best practice (one used repeatedly and successfully by another organization) or to create a new one.

♦ Determining the level of risk and complexity associated with the reengineering effort.

Sometimes there's a misunderstanding about what a vision is. For example, when a company CEO says, "Let's be world-class," this comment does not constitute a vision. It's so vague that it might pertain to any organization.

Instead, a vision needs to be specific and should be stated with conviction. Here's a good working definition of a vision:

> *A vision is the articulation of the image, values, direction, and goals that will guide the future of the organization.*

Henry Ford and his first automobile, known as a "Quadricycle," 1896

An all-too-common error is made when the vision is mistaken for strategy or operating plans. An organization's *strategy* is the result of successfully integrating the vision with strategic thinking. The *operating plan* is the executable portion of the strategic plan.

For example, when Henry Ford set out to build an automobile, that was his vision. When he concluded that he should mass produce it and build it as inexpensively as possible—while paying his workers enough in wages to buy it—that was his strategy.

PROCESS CLUSTER 1.2: IDENTIFYING OPPORTUNITIES

The second process cluster involves identifying process candidates for reengineering. The opportunities for reengineering may represent both long- and near-term situations. Some will be blatantly obvious, while others will be disguised or deeply hidden among departments, age-old management practices, and what amounts to "tribal" knowledge.

The main difficulty in identifying opportunities for process innovation is understanding and acknowledging that individual tasks, which have historically been within the traditional confines of various departments, represent bits and pieces of a process that crosses many departments and levels throughout the organization.

The logical order and natural flow of a particular process was always there. However, segregation of duties and responsibilities combined with hierarchical structures fragmented that process and ultimately obscured it. The key challenge is to identify the tasks that make up a process and form them into tangible reengineering opportunities.

Prioritizing

After processes have been identified as candidates for reengineering, they must be prioritized and the pertinent tasks must be sequenced. Subsequently, the opportunities for process reengineering are connected with the specific goals formulated to carry out the vision. Any that do not help to realize the vision are excluded. Then individual milestones are established for the purpose of measuring the progress of the reengineering project.

The process candidates for reengineering should be prioritized early in the effort and before the reengineering team(s) are formed, because the processes identified for reengineering can and will influence the staffing plan.

Avoiding a Common Mistake

One of the most common mistakes made by organizations is attempting to reengineer too many processes at the same time. A number of financial, business, and timing considerations will limit the number of reengineering projects that can be performed simultaneously.

As a general rule, no more than six reengineering projects should be performed concurrently. A small organization might want to drop its maximum number of concurrent projects to three.

Using Criteria for Selection

Selecting processes for reengineering requires the use of both qualitative and quantitative criteria:

*R*eengineering seeks dramatic improvement in productivity by zeroing in on processes that are central to any business.

Randy Ross

♦ Level of business risk.

♦ Provide competitive advantage.

♦ Duration of effort.

♦ Number of resources.

♦ Timing and schedule.

♦ Cost.

♦ Shareholder and customer value.

♦ Potential for failure.

♦ The ability to create breakthrough results and quantum benefits.

All of these elements should be thoroughly examined. However, the last item listed—the ability to create breakthrough results and quantum benefits—is the most crucial.

Developing the Necessary Knowledge

It's important to develop an understanding of how an existing task is performed. Understanding how work is performed and flows in the current business environment is essential for establishing baselines and designating benchmarks (see Chapter 5) as well as for building the knowledge and credibility necessary to complete reengineering.

It's also important to know the capabilities and overall competence of managers and nonmanagerial personnel. This knowledge will be helpful in identifying transformation issues and in selecting people to lead the reengineering efforts for the processes that are ultimately chosen.

The main challenge in developing an understanding of existing tasks and processes is to avoid embarking on an elaborate exercise to validate present needs, procedures, and structures. Although such an exercise may be interesting, validating how and why things are done as they are in the current environment is inconsequential to the mission of reengineering.

During reengineering, the CEO of Banca di America e di Italia (BAI) had a well-formed idea of his own part in the process: "My role was to act as a defender, so that daily urgencies didn't get in the way of the [reengineering] team's work." [3]

PROCESS CLUSTER 1.3: FORMING AND EDUCATING THE REENGINEERING TEAM(S)

The third process cluster of Phase 1 consists of forming and educating the reengineering team(s). One or more teams may be needed, depending on the size and the situation of the organization involved.

The formation of an effective team is not a casual endeavor. Potential team members must be carefully screened and selected, and a responsive team structure must be established. The essential elements of team formation and education are these:

Those selected must be formally removed from their daily responsibilities. They must be able to redirect their energies into an effective reengineering effort. Ensuring this dedication of effort means realigning the organization to compensate for the loss of the members from their regular duties, training the members in reengineering, and creating and instituting new performance measures linked to participation on the reengineering team(s).

Those selected must undergo rigorous training in process innovation, reengineering, and organizational transformation. (See Chapter 9 for further discussion of training issues as well as the essential roles and characteristics of members.)

The Importance of Environment

"Create the right environment and people will perform," says Anthony Beale, head of European HR (human resources) for J.P. Morgan & Co. The right environment, according to Beale, is one that encourages a willingness to take risks and provides employees with a full range of opportunities. [4]

A proper environment must be created for the team. This environment, consisting of dedicated working space, must support the free and open exchange of ideas and information. It also should serve as a repository of working files and ideas for the reengineering project.

The team's work must get off to a quick start. Team members should be assigned to the effort and fully dedicated to the project virtually immediately. Formally announcing the members of a reengineering team and then delaying actual team formation until individual members are available to work on the project is detrimental not only to the project, but also to the team dynamics. Rapid creation of the team is not only essential to overall team performance, but also demonstrates the organization's commitment to the reengineering project.

The unique human issues associated with the effort must be dealt with. For example, managerial personnel must be assessed in terms of their personal leadership qualities and their potential for assuming expanded roles in the organization, as such roles may develop in the course of reengineering. Nonmanagerial personnel must be evaluated in terms of their abilities to become empowered and to assume greater responsibilities. (In the reengineered enterprise, nonmanagerial personnel are more empowered, are less closely supervised, and have a broader scope of duties. Chapter 9 covers this topic in more detail.)

*F*ormally announcing the team members and then delaying team formation is detrimental to the project.

Effective Team Members Are Effective Workers

Some of the qualities that characterize an effective team member are the same qualities that successful organizations look for when they hire workers. Says Sam Heltman, Toyota's head of personnel, "We seek team members who have the aptitude to absorb the considerable training that inexperienced people will need to absorb to do their jobs, and especially to analyze their work and suggest improvements."[5]

PROCESS CLUSTER 1.4: COMMUNICATING THE VISION AND GAINING COMMITMENT

The fourth process cluster involves educating those directly and indirectly involved in the reengineering project. Communicating the purpose of the effort as well as management's commitment to reinvention is critical.

The initial communication should be delivered by the most senior level of the organization, as information from this level commands immediate attention and carries high credibility.

It is essential that the project focus, objectives, and responsibilities be articulated in a consistent manner throughout the organization and revisited from time to time. Continually managing employee expectations and any misconceptions about reengineering and its objectives is important. Specific emphasis should be placed on conveying expectations, minimizing rumors, reducing anxiety levels, and counteracting inaccurate information.

When employees develop a shared understanding of the concepts and process of reengineering, this understanding can improve the organization's acceptance of reengineering and can facilitate the efforts of the reengineering team(s).

To help ensure the success of reengineering, communicate. To achieve reinvention and transformation, educate.

PROCESS CLUSTER 1.5: ESTABLISHING AN INFRASTRUCTURE

The fifth process cluster of Phase 1 involves the establishment of an overall project infrastructure for managing the reengineering process. This responsibility includes developing and implementing three components: (1) project-management practices and standards, (2) project-status reporting, and (3) integration of quality-assurance methods.

Project management for reengineering involves:

♦ Assessing the business and organizational risks of reengineering certain processes.

♦ Conceptualizing the overall project and its methods and procedures.

♦ Modifying, adapting, and adding to the process clusters and work steps of the five-phase methodology.

♦ Determining appropriate reengineering-team staffing assignments and the estimated level of professional effort to perform each task.

♦ Assessing and prioritizing various process dependencies and critical paths in and among the various processes.

♦ Ensuring the creation, cohesiveness, and effectiveness of the reengineering team(s).

♦ Providing for the periodic communication of the project's status and results.

♦ Implementing project-tracking methods to monitor and manage the flow and progress of work.

♦ Managing the rate of organizational and process change and new-process assimilation.

I've known folks who are constantly relying on someone else for transportation because their cars won't start. They say, "I don't need another car, I just need to fix this one up." Finally, stuck on a stretch of deserted road, perhaps with a howling child or two, they realize the need for a new vehicle. I'd like to see American business avoid that scenario.

Holly S. Slay

Because of the complex nature of a reengineering project and the multitude of activities and processes addressed, a project-management system with a clear and usable structure is absolutely essential to the success of reinvention. In addition, it's essential to develop a detailed work plan that includes steps, tasks, assignments, timelines, deliverables, and the estimated level of effort necessary for performing reengineering.

"For God's sake, Wilburson, will you stop 'touching base'!"

©1993 Henry R. Martin—first published in Harvard Business Review, July/August 1993

CONCLUSION

How did you do at envisioning your own organization in the process of undergoing Phase 1? Did elements of a vision and goals occur to you? Were you able to identify some process candidates for reengineering?

How about people who would make good members for the reengineering team(s)? And how about people from senior management who would be especially good at communicating the vision and gaining commitment?

Did you have any useful ideas about establishing a project infrastructure for managing the reengineering process? Whose knowledge and business savvy would be especially useful in creating an infrastructure?

What about developing the initial work plan? Who are the best planners in your organization?

After your organization has completed Phase 1, it will have laid the foundation for a successful reengineering effort. A carefully devised plan is essential. As you will see when you read the next few chapters covering Phases 2 through 5, a hasty or haphazard approach to Phase 1 would make proceeding impossible.

Bennett Harrison, *author of* Lean and Mean: The Changing Landscape of Corporate Power in the Age of Flexibility, *advocates taking benchmarking one step further to collaboration among rival organizations. Big companies, he suggests, are already working together more closely, both to learn from one another and to reduce the costs of entering new markets and creating leading-edge products. For example, General Motors' joint venture with Toyota Motor Company in Fremont, California, is turning out Geo Prisms and Toyota Corollas that post better quality ratings than cars built in Japan.*[1]

Phase 2: Benchmarking and Defining Success

Company goals should always be geared toward being the best in the world, rather than just slightly better than last year.

Jim Sierk, Vice President of Quality, Xerox Corporation

5

Phase 2 involves intensive work in acquiring information about the practices within and outside the organization. Then, the acquired information must be assessed to determine successful practices that should be adopted and improved on as well as what can and cannot be accomplished during reengineering.

During this phase the reengineering team must stay focused on quantum gains. Therefore, in establishing performance targets the team must strive for at least a 50-percent improvement.

How Do You Choose Areas to Benchmark?

Many companies start off on the wrong foot by making a poor choice about which area to benchmark first. "Most companies benchmark their strongest function against the best-in-class company," says Motorola's Bill Smith. "That's not the most productive approach, though. It's much more beneficial to make major improvements to your weakest functions rather than making smaller improvements to the areas in which you are already strong."[2]

Objectives of Phase 2

♦ **Develop an understanding of the processes to be reengineered and related issues.**

♦ **Establish performance targets for each reengineered process.**

♦ **Select and improve on best practices.**

♦ **Determine what is or is not possible and set meaningful parameters.**

PHASE 2 PROCESS CLUSTERS

Phase 2 consists of four process clusters:

♦ 2.1: Benchmarking Business Practices.

♦ 2.2: Identifying, Copying, and Improving on Best Practices.

♦ 2.3: Assessing Information Technology.

♦ 2.4: Establishing Performance Targets.

These clusters are explained in detail in the following paragraphs.

PROCESS CLUSTER 2.1: BENCHMARKING BUSINESS PRACTICES

The first process cluster of Phase 2 involves benchmarking. David Altany, writing in *Industry Week,* has provided a good definition of "benchmarking": "...measuring and comparing a company's operations, products, and services against those of top performers both within and outside that company's primary industry. The aim of this process is to identify the leading companies' secrets to success, and then...copy them."[3]

A more contemporary interpretation of benchmarking goes a step further. The procedure can be external or internal—outside or inside the organization. Copying other organizations' activities sounds like industrial espionage to some people, but the truth is that benchmarking is perfectly legal and ethical and, according to some enterprises, essential to enhancing competitiveness. In fact, this procedure frequently involves the exchange of information between two organizations, so that both benefit.

Baselining

Benchmarking includes an activity known as "baselining," which means measuring and documenting the flow of activities in a process *as that process is currently performed within the organization doing reengineering.*

> *Baselining involves acquiring quantitative and qualitative information about a process and the functions that support the process.*

In baselining it is essential to use consistent measuring processes, analytical techniques, and definitions so that accurate measurements are made and the resulting conclusions are valid. One of the critical tasks is to determine the value of the process, by assessing not only the work performed during the process, but also the activities preceding and following the process. Factors such as cycle time, number of employees involved, and costs are considered.

As a result of the assessment, the reengineering team develops an understanding of the value of current activities to the enterprise and its customers, as that value relates to the vision, direction, and objectives of the reengineering effort.

Baselining also helps in identifying goals for improvement. Accurate baseline data are compared to valid internal or external measures. These measures can be related to similar processes performed either by other divisions and parts of the organization or by external entities. The external entities can be industry peers, competitors, or organizations in different industries.

Internal vs. External Benchmarking

Internal benchmarking is used to compare one department, process, or practice within the organization to another. External benchmarking is more complicated, as it is used to

As managers become more confident about benchmarking, they can readily extend it beyond cost reduction to profit-producing factors like service levels and customer satisfaction.[4]

compare a practice used by the organization doing reengineering to a practice of another enterprise.

In external benchmarking the organization's practices can be compared either to those of its peers or chief competitors, or to those of organizations that are neither peers nor competitors.

The Difficulties of Benchmarking

Although benchmarking is extremely useful, it presents some difficulties that you need to be aware of:

♦ Benchmarking provides information about the *quantitative* characteristics of a particular task or series of tasks, but very little information about its *qualitative* attributes.

♦ Comparing baseline performance measurements to the performance of external organizations requires gathering information and analyzing data in a consistent manner (by always applying the same rules, terms, and standards). All too frequently a reengineering team arrives at erroneous or premature conclusions based on incompatible measurement methods.

♦ Data from benchmarking often contain errors. Benchmarks and their statistical profiles pertain to how things are done today, not to processes as they will be after they have been reengineered. And it's extremely difficult to compare benchmarks of existing processes to the potential results of reengineering.

PROCESS CLUSTER 2.2: IDENTIFYING, COPYING, AND IMPROVING ON BEST PRACTICES

In certain reengineering projects, identifying and copying best practices may be appropriate. "Best practices" are probably what David Altany meant when he mentioned "secrets to success" in his definition of "benchmarking" presented earlier in this chapter.

> *Best practices are those that are*
> *considered to be premiere, world class, or*
> *without peer.*

The decision to use a best practice in reengineering should be based on the answers to three questions:

- ♦ Does the practice provide an immediate competitive advantage that is both measurable and discernible?
- ♦ Does the practice optimize shareholder value or the benefits of performing that practice, compared to cost and effort?
- ♦ Does the practice provide a useful model for all organizations engaged in that practice, not just competitors or members of the same industry?

If the members of the reengineering team can answer "yes" to all three questions, then we suggest that they choose the practice, learn everything they can about it, improve on it, and do it differently to create a competitive advantage.

Developing knowledge about a best practice usually means analyzing the management techniques, responsibilities, and objectives of the organization that employs the best practice. Once this thorough understanding has been achieved, the team can begin to make the best practice even more effective.

PROCESS CLUSTER 2.3: ASSESSING INFORMATION TECHNOLOGY

The objective of the third process cluster is to assess the status, capabilities, effectiveness, and orientation of the organization's information technology as they relate to the vision and strategy of the reinvented enterprise. Here are the steps involved:

♦ Determining where the organization is in the evolution of its information technology.

♦ Ascertaining where information technology should be to best support the organization's reengineering imperatives.

♦ Evaluating whether the organization should or can evolve naturally, accelerate its evolution, or leapfrog to a higher level.

In determining priorities and the organization's ability to transform itself with the support of technology, the reengineering team needs to figure out whether technology can help provide enabling solutions in a cost-effective and timely manner. The issues involved are these:

♦ The current and future sophistication of technology.

♦ The level of integration of technology into the day-to-day life of the organization.

♦ The software applications that are available in the marketplace.

♦ Ways to obtain and use data.

♦ Employees' attitudes toward technology.

PROCESS CLUSTER 2.4: ESTABLISHING PERFORMANCE TARGETS

The final process cluster consists of:

♦ Assessing the behaviors connected with the processes that were baselined and benchmarked earlier.

♦ Selecting (if appropriate) any best practice that is to be copied and improved on.

CONCLUSION

It is not uncommon for a successful reengineering effort to achieve improvements of two, three, or five times the baseline level of a process. For example, one of our efforts reduced order-fulfillment time from one and one-half days to less than one hour.

If a process is incapable of yielding the minimum return, then it's not a candidate for reengineering. Thus, you can see how important it is to establish meaningful performance targets, as these targets help to further define and structure the objectives of reinvention.

Writing in **Time**, *John Greenwald describes General Electric's three-day "workout" sessions in which workers and managers meet on anything from gripes to pitches for new products. On the third day the employees make scores of suggestions. Once, in a session at an aircraft-engine plant, a team pitched a plan that cut the time needed to produce a jet-combustion part nearly 90 percent. And an electrician proposed an aluminum reflector that subsequently cut the plant's light bill in half. These workouts have spawned dozens of innovations, ranging from improved light-bulb packaging to the elimination of reams of paperwork.*[1]

PHASE 3: INNOVATING PROCESSES

*One thing that makes one company better
than another is ideas.*

Don Bagin and Frank Grazian,
writing in *Communication Briefings*

6

Phase 3 is the essence of organizational reinvention through process reengineering. It's the most demanding phase of our methodology, as it requires not only the reengineering of business processes, but also the systemic change of management practices, organizational structures, and information technology.

Reengineering a process may consist of such methods as developing a way to adopt, improve on, and implement a "best practice" or creating a brand-new process. It's best to trust the reengineering team's judgment on which is a better approach in a particular instance.

If we did all the things we are capable of doing, we would literally astonish ourselves.

Thomas Edison

Objectives of Phase 3

- **The members of the reengineering team create new processes, each of which:**
- **Reduces the time needed to complete the process.**
- **Eliminates low-value work.**
- **Increases productivity.**
- **Achieves the quantum results planned during Phase 2.**
- **Optimizes the value of the process to shareholders.**

PHASE 3 PROCESS CLUSTERS

Phase 3 is organized into six process clusters:

- 3.1: Conceptualizing the Process.
- 3.2: Mapping the Process.
- 3.3: Testing the Prototype Process.
- 3.4: Refining the Prototype Process.
- 3.5: Reengineering the Information Technology.
- 3.6: Substituting the New Process for the Old One.

In this chapter we speak as though only one reengineering project (process, practice, or structure) is being undertaken, but of course that won't necessarily be the case. Any number of reengineering projects may be undertaken, and it's possible that each will have its own reengineering team. However, we find it easier to explain Phase 3 by discussing the steps to be taken with a single project.

PROCESS CLUSTER 3.1: CONCEPTUALIZING THE PROCESS

Generating Ideas

Ultimately, the reengineering of a process is the product of the reengineering team's creativity and boldness. The members may employ any of a number of techniques in generating ideas: They may use a best practice as a model; they may hit on something by trial and error; they may "import" a process from another part of the organization; or they may invent something entirely new.

The members may even go beyond their organization's geographical, industrial, and physical boundaries. For example, innovation, operational excellence, and competitive advantage may be achieved by creating synergistic partnerships with other organizations or relationships with customers.

The key is for the team to recognize good ideas, formulate them within the context of the objectives of the reengineering vision, and determine whether they represent viable concepts to pursue.

Developing an innovative process requires thinking broadly and outside the usual context. The team members must be willing to explore, experiment, fail, refine ideas, and try again until they have a seamless process that contributes to a more effective organization.

Writing a Process Description

The team must write a description of the way in which the process will be organized and performed in the "real-world" environment. Such a description is important in conveying the concept to others and in creating a tangible link between the vision, the concept of the reengineered process, and its physical operation.

The written description not only defines the new process, but also explains the assumptions under which it will be performed and its expected results. This description is then tested against the opportunities and baselines developed in Phase 2.

PROCESS CLUSTER 3.2: MAPPING THE PROCESS

The second cluster involves creating a map of the reengineered process. A process map illustrates the design of the process, including how the work will be organized and how

DILBERT® by Scott Adams

DILBERT® reprinted by permission of UFS, Inc.

Just as a blueprint is used to construct a building, a process map is used to construct a process.

personnel and technology will be involved. These are the specific elements that a process map depicts:

♦ What activities are performed.

♦ How they are performed.

♦ How they are sequenced.

♦ How the work flows.

♦ How much time is consumed during and between various activities.

♦ What areas of the organization are responsible for various activities.

♦ How information technology is to be used.

Developing a Series of Maps

Just as a blueprint is used to construct a building, a process map is used to construct a process. Reengineering a process, like constructing a building, is complex and incorporates many elements. But if too much information is included in a single map, people may become confused or overwhelmed.

Consequently, it's helpful to develop a series of process maps representing increasing levels of information about the process. In this way, people can become acquainted with the most basic map before they are introduced to one with more information, and another with even more information, and so on.

Generally, there are four levels of process maps:

Level 1: Enterprise Activities (EAs). Enterprise activities are ones that are similar, involve a number of different organizational areas, and are essential to the enterprise.

Level 2: Essential Core Activities (ECAs). Essential core activities are those that are critical to enterprise activities.

Involving a number of operational activities, organizational levels, and management practices, they are processes that simply must be performed. Examples of ECAs include performing a credit review and authorization, scheduling appointments with carriers, and production planning.

UPI/Bettmann

An example of a process activity. Process maps include descriptions of such activities.

Level 3: Primary Core Activities (PCAs). Primary core activities are ones that are required to perform the essential core activities.

Level 4: Elemental Process Activities (EPAs). EPAs are the most discrete level of detail included in the process map. They are finite tasks and work steps that are required to support a primary core activity. An example of an EPA is choosing a certain quantity and type of product to ship to customers.

When process maps are developed using these four levels, they provide a clear and consistent representation of what the reengineered process will look like and how it will be performed. The four-level approach also enables a wide variety of people to use the maps in the implementation of the process.

Comparing Process Maps to Baseline, Vision, and Goals

The maps of the reengineered process are compared to the baseline for the current process (developed in Phase 2). The comparison should provide evidence of:

- ◆ Fewer activities involved in the process.
- ◆ Less fragmentation of work, so that work flows in a natural, less complicated sequence.

G**TE will spend
$50 million over
the next few years
on training that
helps managers
adapt their skills
and styles to a
leaner, flatter
organization.²**

♦ Faster completion of the process and its activities.

♦ Fewer checks, balances, and reconciliation efforts.

♦ Fewer transfers of the process from one person or function to another; less human intervention.

♦ Lower transaction costs.

♦ Higher value.

♦ Fewer organizational levels involved.

In addition to comparing the process maps to the baseline, the team validates the maps against the overall reengineering vision and goals established in Phase 1. This validation not only ensures that expectations are being met, but also allows team members to assess their ability to develop innovative processes and their ability to work together as an effective unit.

Identifying Responsible Areas of the Organization

In creating the process maps, the team identifies the areas of the organization responsible for the process and the number of personnel needed to complete the activities involved. As part of the identification procedure, the team consolidates a number of activities into a single process and compresses the organizational hierarchy.

Staffing requirements and productivity levels of individual employees are also assessed. This assessment results in an initial estimate of the number and types of skills that will be necessary to support the new process.

PROCESS CLUSTER 3.3: TESTING THE PROTOTYPE PROCESS

The third process cluster, testing the prototype process, is based on the process maps. The prototype is used in a simulation based on a set of environmental assumptions.

Testing the process offers the organization a number of benefits:

♦ It creates a managed environment in which the new process can be analyzed.

♦ It facilitates the introduction of the new process and any related organizational change.

♦ It allows the reengineering team to assess the validity and viability of goals, projections, and objectives.

♦ It enables the team to estimate the implications of reengineering with a high level of precision. The estimates can then be compared to the original goals and measurements developed in Phase 2 and adjusted as necessary.

♦ It allows the prototype to be tested by those who will be responsible for using the process successfully.

PROCESS CLUSTER 3.4: REFINING THE PROTOTYPE PROCESS

The fourth process cluster consists of refining the process and preparing it for implementation. Refinement, which is based on the results obtained during the prototype test, can involve many activities ranging from the fine-tuning of the process to the complete redesign of the process and its maps.

Refinement may involve additional training, more organizational changes, and alteration of management practices. The refining of a process also may allow for the introduction of other new processes and organizational changes that further facilitate the transformation process.

PROCESS CLUSTER 3.5: REENGINEERING THE INFORMATION TECHNOLOGY

In the process of reinvention, most organizations must reengineer not only their organizational processes and structures, but also their technological resources. The fifth process cluster consists of developing the technological architecture to support reengineering—a cross-functional task requiring profound rethinking, a departure from previous uses of

Radical surgery is needed in IS processes. One of the first ideas that will have to go is the whole notion of traditional systems development life cycles.

Michael Hammer

technology, and a change in management's approach to technology.

The organization's technology must offer capabilities that enable reengineering. The technology should be devised according to a common standard and should be integrated, transportable, and scalable. And the necessary technological capabilities must be delivered *quickly,* not in two or three years—a serious challenge for the information-systems (IS) function.

Our model includes six steps for creating a new technological architecture to support the reengineered enterprise:

Step 1: Visioning information technology. To be successful at reengineering, the enterprise must have a clear definition of what it is and a clear vision of what it wants to be, combined with the information technology to support its initiatives. In this step the reengineering team concentrates on envisioning the technology that needs to exist in order to take the organization where it wants to go.

Step 2: Determining drivers. Most organizations, regardless of size, find that six to fifteen major influences drive their efforts to reengineer their information technology. Some of the more common drivers are:

♦ Customer demands.

♦ Competitor initiatives and business practices.

♦ Internal operational requirements.

♦ Shareholder mandates.

♦ Technological developments.

Identification of drivers is critical. These drivers form the planning assumptions, strategic tenets, and principles on which the architecture of the reengineered technology will be based.

What Drove Three Firms to Reengineering[3]

	Reengineering Goals	Challenges for IS	Solution
Texas Instruments Inc.	To better deal with demands for quicker product development and delivery cycle times in businesses such as semi-conductors and defense systems.	To respond quickly enough with new applications and support for business process reengineering.	Began extensive training for all in IS. Reorganized IS into centers of excellence. Changed IS employee rewards to emphasize breadth of technical knowledge and performance.
Elf Atochem Inc.	To rationalize the merger of three chemical companies into one.	To break with the old pattern of automating existing processes.	Created dedicated business-consulting group within IS. Concentrated on improved communication with business.
California State Automobile Association	To improve customer service, cut operating expenses, prepare for changes in government regulation.	Poor reputation with customers. Not considered central part of reengineering team.	Improved record for delivering applications on time. Revamped information architecture.

Determining information-technology drivers involves:

1. Finding the "best practices" in the arena of information technology and figuring out the appropriateness of those practices for a reengineering effort.

2. Identifying valid reengineering opportunities that are predicated on information technology.

3. Ascertaining the specific requirements or the measurable objectives of the process.

4. Honestly and realistically evaluating existing information-technology capabilities and resources.

5. Defining and prioritizing the information-technology needs of both external and internal customers.

6. Understanding the technological objectives and needs of business partners.

Step 3: Conducting a comparative assessment of information technology. It's important to realize that not all of the organization's existing technology and the organizational structures associated with that technology can support reengineering. The objective of this step is to identify the gap between how existing technology is used and how technology will need to be used during reengineering and in the reinvented organization.

> **Information technology must allow the**
> **organization to meet its emerging needs**
> **as defined by its identified drivers.**

Consequently, during this step the reengineering team prioritizes the drivers according to their influence on the information-technology architecture. Gaps are not only identified, but also evaluated and put in order according to how critical they are.

Step 4: Forming an information-technology strategy and validating the vision for information technology . During this step a long-range strategy for information technology is developed. This strategy is tested against the five essential elements (see Chapter 1, "Five Elements of Reengineering"), the vision for the reinvented enterprise, and the drivers of information technology.

Step 5: Identifying, defining, and prioritizing the application systems required to enable reengineering. The major issue for many organizations is to find those application systems that support process innovation and functional consolidation and provide competitive advantage.

The 5th Wave by Rich Tennant

"We're using a 4-tiered system—PC, to mini, to Mr. Smoothy, to mainframe."

©The 5th Wave by Rich Tennant, Rockport, MA

Many reengineering efforts are hampered by older systems that support traditional processes and responsibilities that disappear during the process of reengineering. Also, because many of these systems are inflexible, changing them is both difficult and expensive.

Yet, in reengineering, technology is the enabling agent. Systems need to be accessible to end-users and highly adaptable to rapidly changing needs. Consequently, a new information-technology architecture must be developed and installed.

We envision this architecture as consisting of three tiers:

♦ Mainframes for massive, homogeneous needs.

♦ Midrange alternatives (for example, AS/400 or VAX) for less intensive transaction-processing needs.

♦ Client-server/integrated work stations for highly specialized needs.

All three tiers should be networked and seamlessly integrated to provide common access to data and programs.

The trademarks of this environment will be electronic mail, integrated voice and video communications, a common look and feel to organization-wide applications through graphical user interfaces, and the creation of a common work environment through concepts such as groupware. Applications and data will be scalable, portable, and interchangeable.

Step 6: Transforming information technology. The transformation from the old technology to the organization's new technological architecture requires careful planning of related timing, schedules, and procedures and usually results in significant organizational change. The reengineering team addresses the financial requirements of the transformation, the internal and external resources that will be needed, and the issues involved with conversion from one computer system to another.

PROCESS CLUSTER 3.6: SUBSTITUTING THE NEW PROCESS FOR THE OLD ONE

The final process cluster is the preparation of the new process for implementation: ensuring that the necessary infrastructure, procedures, and systems are in place and ready.

To Innovate, Just Ask

Frisby, a supplier of hydraulic subsystems and assemblies to aircraft manufacturers, wanted to reinvent itself. CEO Greg Frisby explains what happened:

"What we did was get back to the same entrepreneurial spirit that was there when [my father Ray] started the place, and the same reliance on our employees as empowered decision makers."

When the organization asked its employees to come up with ideas for significantly lowering the cost of a job, Greg notes that "it was incredible, the number of suggestions and the wealth of information. They had been waiting for this moment."[4]

CONCLUSION

Phase 3 is about innovation. Sometimes organizations make the mistake of assuming that employees can't innovate. Consider this comment from a custodian being honored on the occasion of his retirement: "You blew it. For twenty-five years all you got were my hands; for the same salary you could have had my brains."[5]

People have wonderful ideas and enormous potential. What they need is positive leadership to cultivate their potential, encouragement to voice their ideas, and continuing support as they follow through on their own creativity.

Without a desire to learn and the skills to do so, what will happen to the employees of the 21st Century? They will be trampled by the pace of change, according to Alan Downs, writing in Training magazine. Downs suggests that the key employee trait will be a willingness to learn. With it, employees will be more likely to adapt as their jobs change and to experience change as a challenge to be mastered. They will flex and grow, thereby ensuring their own success and the success of the organization.[1]

PHASE 4: TRANSFORMING THE ORGANIZATION

*The success of process reengineering lies not only in
executing a well-defined methodology, or in
developing leading-edge technology, or in structuring
a set of human resource enablers, but in actually
moving the organization to implement the changes.*

John Farrell, writing in *Planning Review*

7

In Phase 4 the organization is transformed into the reengineered enterprise. As we've mentioned before, changing an established organization with long-standing beliefs and practices is a risky and difficult task. Employees must be both *able* and *willing* to function in their new environment; otherwise, the vision of reengineering simply will not materialize. This means that they must be educated about the reengineered enterprise, empowered so that they can work effectively, and willing to assume the responsibilities and burdens of change.

It's important to remember that resistance to change is a natural instinct, but when left unchecked it can result in complete reversion to former practices.

In a study of 1,000 organizations' quality-improvement efforts, more than 35 percent of respondents reported stiff resistance and outright sabotage.[2]

Objectives of Phase 4

♦ **Ensure that organizational operations are consistent with the processes that have been reengineered.**

♦ **Create a leaner, flatter, and more agile organizational structure.**

♦ **Foster empowerment so that employees are able to function effectively in the reengineered organization.**

♦ **Ensure that employees are prepared and willing to carry out the reengineered processes.**

♦ **Implement the processes developed in Phase 3.**

PHASE 4 PROCESS CLUSTERS

Phase 4 has three process clusters:

♦ 4.1: Transforming Operations.

♦ 4.2: Transforming Organizational Structures.

♦ 4.3: Implementing Reengineered Processes.

PROCESS CLUSTER 4.1: TRANSFORMING OPERATIONS

The transformation of operations—changing methods, practices, and procedures—occurs primarily as a result of innovating and reengineering processes and technology. However, operations should be examined carefully after reinvention to determine whether further changes and refinements are essential for successful process implementation.

PROCESS CLUSTER 4.2: TRANSFORMING ORGANIZATIONAL STRUCTURES

Transforming organizational structures includes building employee empowerment and creating a leaner, flatter, and more agile enterprise. The key assumptions of this process cluster are:

♦ Human beings continually evolve and learn.

♦ They can be encouraged to evolve into empowered workers who make decisions on their own.

♦ The organization can gain competitive advantage through excellence.

Prescription for Fostering Empowerment and Decision Making [3]

Ingredient #1: Encouragement

Many people have worked only in organizations that concentrate decision making at the upper levels. Consequently, they need to be encouraged to speak up, suggest changes, and experiment with decision making.

Ingredient #2: Responsibility

In an empowering organization, the responsibility for making a decision is made at the organizational level or location that is most appropriate in terms of information, expertise, and need. A bonus of this approach: People who participate in making a decision feel a heightened responsibility for ensuring a successful outcome.

Ingredient #3: Training

Workers must receive training for assuming the increased responsibility of decision making. Asking them to make decisions without the relevant understanding and experience is counterproductive.

Ingredient #4: Guidelines

Because speed is often a critical factor in making a decision, management must lay the groundwork in advance by devising and conveying effective guidelines that delineate not only the decision-making participants, but also the method of decision making under a number of different circumstances.

Ingredient #5: A Developmental Perspective

When an organization views a decision as one entity—from recognition to planning to implementing to evaluating to generalizing—it has an easier time instituting a more open and participative decision-making process.

The transformation process consists of three steps:

Step 1: Designing the reinvented organization. This step consists of reengineering management and organizational structures to support the reinvented enterprise. Performance goals and measurements are also developed to support the new organization and its role.

The reengineering team must create not only a design plan, but also physical models that illustrate how the new organization will be structured and how its human resources will be aligned. These models should include:

♦ The organizational structures themselves.

♦ Spans of control.

♦ Numbers of employees needed.

♦ Behavioral characteristics that employees must have to implement the reengineered enterprise.

♦ The names of key change agents who may be able to help in implementation.

The models guide implementation and can also be used to help prioritize employee needs for education, assistance, and information technology.

Step 2: Performing a comparative assessment. This step is a comprehensive assessment of the abilities of the existing organization (both structure and personnel) to satisfy the projected requirements of the reinvented

After months of study, management reveals the new reorganization plan.

enterprise. The primary purpose is to identify gaps between current capabilities and the demands of newly reengineered processes. Once gaps have been identified, the severity of each is evaluated and a determination is made regarding priorities and the best methods to address gaps and priorities.

Step 3: Developing a change-management plan. The change-management plan, which is based on the results of the comparative assessment, is a detailed plan of action for realizing organizational transformation. The plan addresses a wide range of issues:

♦ Announcing the transformation to customers, partners, and shareholders.

♦ Sharing information about the transformation with employees.

♦ Establishing a training program for the employees.

♦ Devising transition schedules.

♦ Establishing a method for conveying information about the reengineering effort, as needed, throughout the implementation period.

♦ Specifying the new organizational structure, the related requirements for staffing, and the new system of measuring and rewarding performance (which should be linked to the implementation of reengineering).

Perhaps the most important part of the plan is an effective approach to training employees. Typically, the training involves four steps:

*W*hen you make a major change, you create a kind of corporate vacuum while employees wait to see what happens. The trick is to fill that vacuum with positive ideas before others fill it with negative ones.

Barry Gibbons

How NOT to Introduce Change

Many companies follow a sure-fire method for creating resistance to change: They try to force it down employees' throats. Often the CEO calls a company-wide meeting and informs people of the new path that the company has decided to follow.

"When senior management justifies a change...like that and then walks away thinking it's done its job, [it has] really missed the boat," says William Bridges, author of numerous books on change.[4]

1. General orientation.

2. The details of completing each reengineered process (for those who will perform that process).

3. The use of newly reengineered technology.

4. The behavior that's appropriate for functioning in the new enterprise.

Because reengineering is unique for every organization, the exact training required to orient and educate employees is also unique.

The Impact of Employee Training

Greyhound Lines Inc., the Chicago-based bus company, requires all new employees who work with customers to take "reality training." This course casts trainees in the role of customers and forces them to endure realistic simulations of actual service failures that have happened on occasion to customers of Greyhound.

One month after "reality training" began, Greyhound realized a 50-percent decrease in customer complaints. The company hadn't changed any procedures for dealing with service failures, but employees who received the training were much more empathic and understanding of customer problems. They simply exhibited a better attitude than employees who had not received the training.[5]

PROCESS CLUSTER 4.3: IMPLEMENTING REENGINEERED PROCESSES

The implementation of reengineered processes depends on successfully managing change and the rate of change. A multitude of change agents must be managed. These agents generally affect the organization in four areas:

♦ Leadership.

♦ Infrastructure.

♦ Transformation.

♦ Business processes.

Typical change agents include:

♦ CEO communication.

♦ Employee involvement as well as empowerment.

♦ Creativity/process innovation.

♦ Commitment to change.

♦ Education and training.

CONCLUSION

At this point of the reengineering journey, the organization has changed its orientation, committed to new processes, developed innovations, created new attitudes and ways of thinking, designed and tested new processes, and redeveloped and perfected other processes. Now it is poised to implement processes and thereby transform itself into a reinvented enterprise.

Both expectations and anxiety will be high. People need to be reassured and reminded that:

◆ In essence, they've already reengineered.

◆ Those who have reengineered processes have set the organization on the right course for success in the future.

◆ Those who will help to implement a new or redeveloped process will turn the organization's vision into reality.

In a successful organization, the commitment to innovation extends beyond the reengineering project and becomes a way of life. According to Michael Michalko, writing in Training & Development, *innovative thinking can be generated by letting employees know that they're allowed to fail. He suggests asking employees to identify the organization's three biggest failures in the past three years. If they can't, the organization isn't experimenting enough.*[1]

Phase 5: Monitoring Reengineered Processes

We're starting to institutionalize dissatisfaction, not with a lot of phony breast-beating and vows to do better, but by recognizing the professional satisfaction and intellectual fun that come with figuring out how to refine a process, take it up to a new level, and then start all over again to take it up one more level.

Robert Eaton, CEO of Chrysler Corporation

8

Phase 5 consists of establishing an ongoing procedure for monitoring and adjusting reengineered processes and their respective support structures. Although every reengineering project comes to a conclusion, the commitment to innovate processes, enhance value, and achieve competitive advantage must continue.

PHASE 5 PROCESS CLUSTERS

There are three process clusters in Phase 5:

- ♦ 5.1: Refining Processes.
- ♦ 5.2: Monitoring for Improvement.
- ♦ 5.3: Transferring Learning.

Objectives of Phase 5

♦ Evaluate reengineered processes and adjust as needed.
♦ Evaluate the organization's opportunities for improvement.
♦ Extend learning from reengineering to other organizational areas and practices.

PROCESS CLUSTER 5.1: REFINING PROCESSES

This process cluster consists of assessing the effectiveness of reengineered processes. All new processes are reviewed periodically to ensure that they are providing quantum results. Such reviews not only allow for refinements to be made, but also ensure that the reengineered processes are consistently linked to the organization's vision and goals.

PROCESS CLUSTER 5.2: MONITORING FOR IMPROVEMENT

After the conclusion of the formal reengineering effort, the organization must continually evaluate itself and its opportunities for improvement. This kind of evaluation goes far beyond quality issues and financial performance. It includes the challenge to improve on management practices, organizational effectiveness, and employee empowerment.

A New Way to Look at Competition[2]

Old Paradigm	*New Paradigm*
The "others" are my enemy.	The "others" are my benchmark.
The name of the game is winning.	The name of the game is continual development.
I am better than they are.	I am important.
I am separate from the others.	I am part of the community.

PROCESS CLUSTER 5.3: TRANSFERRING LEARNING

Transferring learning requires a commitment to extending what has been learned from the reengineering effort to other parts of the organization and other practices. Reengineered processes that could be used in other functions are identified, evaluated, and selectively modified. This transference increases the returns obtained from reengineering.

Another bonus is that the organization can extend what it has learned to its customers, suppliers, business partners, and associates. Every reengineered enterprise should trade information with those who can provide input leading to synergy, greater operational excellence, and better competitive advantage. In this way organizations can share not only knowledge, but also technology, practices, and perhaps even selected personnel.

CONCLUSION

By this time the organization has acquired the skills necessary to set up and run an ongoing program for evaluating and improving on reengineered processes, monitoring success, and acting on opportunities for improvement. Reengineering has left the organization enriched in a way that will continue to have an effect in the future—as long as employees are motivated, encouraged to use their creativity, supported by top management, and rewarded for their efforts.

The subject of the next chapter is the one most critical to the success of any reengineering effort— managing human issues effectively.

Beverly Geber, writing in Training *magazine, suggests that there are some general ways to describe companies that are successful in the long term…. High-performance workplaces invest in the skills of their workers by providing lots of training, and they make sure those workers have ample opportunities on the job to hone existing skills and develop new ones. They align the economic interests of workers with the company through programs such as gain-sharing or employee ownership. High-performance workplaces also are characterized by a willingness to share operational and financial information with employees. And they provide employees with some say about their jobs.*[1]

THE HUMAN SIDE
OF REENGINEERING

*If you're not thinking all the time about making every person
more valuable, you don't have a chance.*

Jack Welch, CEO of General Electric

9

Now that we've described our model for reengineering,
we concentrate on the issue that is the greatest determinant
of success in applying that model: managing the human
resources involved.

A number of questions must be answered:

♦ How do you staff a reengineering effort?

♦ Does the organization need the help of an external
consultant to perform reengineering?

♦ How might employees react to the effort?

♦ How will employees' work lives differ in the reengineered enterprise?

In this chapter we offer answers to these questions and
present our view of the human issues that will confront an

organization as it embarks on, wends its way through, and ultimately completes the reengineering journey.

STAFFING A REENGINEERING EFFORT

As each reengineering effort is unique to the enterprise, there is no exact formula for the number of reengineering teams required, the number of members per team, or the number of people needed to support organizational transformation.

However, it is necessary to have the following individuals or groups to support and manage the reengineering effort, coordinate resources and personnel, and transform the organization:

♦ Executive Sponsors.

♦ Reinvention Steering Committee.

♦ Transformation Leader.

♦ Process Champion.

♦ Reengineering Team(s).

As we explain in the paragraphs that follow, all of these people or groups have specific roles. After discussing these roles, we present another that we believe to be essential to successful reengineering: the role of an external consultant.

EXECUTIVE SPONSORS

The executive sponsors are from the highest level of the organization: the chief executive officer (CEO), the chief financial officer

---

Communication During Reengineering

Managers must approach communication as an interpersonal activity. To memos and videos add a half-day off-site followed by a casual lunch, small-group meetings of employees and their managers, and town-hall meetings with senior executives. Managers must give employees sound reasons for and explanations of the new design, a forum for voicing concerns, and feedback to show those concerns are being heard.[2]

(CFO), and the chief operating officer (COO). Because of their authority, stature, and commitment, these sponsors are able to:

- ◆ Endorse the reengineering effort.

- ◆ Provide it with direction.

- ◆ Set its tone.

- ◆ Instill motivation in those involved.

- ◆ Assist in surmounting organizational barriers, overcoming turf issues, dealing with personalities, and letting go of doctrines.

- ◆ Continually exhibit their passion for creating quantum gains.

General Electric's Jack Welch

Daily responsibilities for the sponsors can be delegated to a senior vice president acting under the direct authority of the CEO.

REINVENTION STEERING COMMITTEE

The steering committee is composed of senior operational managers and selected internal experts who represent a broad spectrum of the enterprise. The responsibilities of the committee are to:

- ◆ Establish reengineering strategies and policies.

- ◆ Eliminate or at least create ways to circumvent barriers to reengineering.

- ◆ Ensure that resources are available and applied.

- ◆ Make sure that process innovation and reengineering are actually taking place.

- ◆ Maintain consistency in the direction of the reengineering effort.

- ◆ Resolve issues regarding the scope and impact of the reengineering effort.

Because this committee offers a forum for candid discussion of any issue affecting the reengineering effort, its function is crucial to the communication and consensus building required during reengineering.

TRANSFORMATION LEADER

The transformation leader guides the organization through the reengineering journey. These are the responsibilities associated with this role:

♦ Establish practices and procedures for reengineering.

♦ Oversee, manage, and coordinate all of the different reengineering projects.

♦ Serve as a source of knowledge about reengineering and organizational transformation.

♦ Educate the reengineering team(s) and process champions in how to perform reengineering.

♦ Design and implement the reengineering infrastructure, including methods for managing projects, standards for reporting progress and results, and documentation for managing reinvention.

♦ Identify and resolve daily project-management issues as necessary.

♦ Evaluate the effectiveness of individual members of the reengineering team and their contributions to the reengineering effort.

♦ Report project status and progress to the executive sponsors and the reinvention steering committee.

The leader can be either an employee with a proven track record of success in organizational transformation or an external consultant. (See the section entitled "The Role of an External Consultant" on page 97.) It is absolutely essential that this person have not only a thorough understanding of the direction that the organization wants to pursue, but also extensive knowledge about how to manage reengineering.

PROCESS CHAMPION

The champion is responsible for the reengineering of a specific process. This person is a senior manager who currently has direct operating responsibility and accountability for that process.

Under prevailing organizational paradigms, many different people have responsibility for various parts of a process. The process champion, though, is the one who's responsible for the daily management of the reengineering team that works in his or her process area.

The process champion has two major responsibilities:

♦ Serve as the project manager of the reengineering team addressing a particular process.

♦ Work in conjunction with the transformation leader.

These responsibilities require abundant energy, charisma, a passion for results, and an organization-wide perspective.

REENGINEERING TEAM(S)

The mission of the reengineering team is to identify and follow through on reinvention opportunities so that competitive advantage and shareholder value can be enhanced. As we mentioned elsewhere, an organization may have one or a number of teams, depending on its size and situation.

A reengineering team is generally staffed with three to seven people—never more than ten.

Team members are or quickly become experts in the reengineering process. However, assigning multiple processes to a single team is not advisable, as it can dilute a team's effectiveness.

Generally, a team is staffed with three to seven people—never more than ten. Too many people can lead to problems with interpersonal relations, personalities, communication, divergent objectives, and so on.

The team members are chosen from areas across the organization, and the team is designed so that its members' skills complement one another. In the course of a reinvention journey, team members will function in a variety of roles. During any portion of the project, a member may be a task leader, an analyst, or the team leader.

Team-Member Characteristics

Not every team member will have all of the abilities and attributes that might characterize an "ideal" member. Nevertheless, a number of abilities and attributes must be represented on the team so that its members can perform reengineering effectively and develop synergy and harmony. The team must:

"Fred has managed to maintain his rugged individualism while functioning as a team player."

♦ Have specific knowledge of the process that is to be reengineered.

♦ Understand the organization's vision, direction, and competitive position.

♦ Be creative.

♦ Be adaptable.

♦ Be able to assimilate new ideas, responsibilities, and roles quickly.

♦ Be able to assess the rationale and the value of work.

♦ Enjoy a challenge.

♦ Have high energy.

♦ Be able to contribute under significant pressure.

♦ Be able and willing to challenge existing procedures.

♦ Be able to comprehend complex business issues and their implications.

In addition, every member must be personally committed to the process of innovation and radical transformation, must be able to work effectively with the other members, and must be open-minded. The team cannot be expected to carry the burden of people who dwell on past problems or perpetuate "war stories" about approaches that have failed, regardless of how skilled these people might be.

The team must be able to work within the organization in a free and unrestricted manner. For many team members, the ability to transcend organizational boundaries and critically examine processes across departments will be a new and sometimes intimidating experience.

Also, especially in the beginning, the team members may be overwhelmed by the magnitude and responsibilities of reengineering, the opportunities presented, and the task of removing traditional organizational barriers. The executive sponsors should communicate fully with the members and assure them that they have management's full support.

THE ROLE OF AN EXTERNAL CONSULTANT

Although there are obvious advantages to using only internal resources in staffing reengineering, efforts that are staffed in this way appear to have a greater tendency toward failure. An exclusively internal staff may:

♦ Be distracted by problems in individual functional areas.

♦ Succumb to self-serving interests.

♦ Be inhibited by organizational boundaries, titles, or politics.

Embedded knowledge in the organization does not just happen. You have to train people in new skills. And you have to constantly upgrade those skills.

C.K. Prahalad

The leader's character is made up of a tripod of forces: ambition and drive; competence and expertise; integrity and moral fabric. All three are needed, and all three have to be in balance, or the tripod topples.

Get a leader with only drive but not competence and integrity, and you get a demagogue.

Get someone with competence but absent integrity and drive, and you get a technocrat.

Get seduced by someone who has ambition and competence but lacks integrity, and you get a destructive achiever.[3]

♦ Be linked to hidden agendas.

♦ Lack the specific skills and knowledge required to perform reengineering.

♦ Underestimate the effort, extent, and magnitude of reengineering.

♦ Lack the perspective to question processes and traditional doctrine.

♦ Lack the knowledge and experience to appreciate the organization's vision and competitive position.

♦ Seek only incremental gains by using tried-and-true methods.

♦ Fall victim to inertia.

Although these tendencies are admittedly natural, they can destroy a reengineering effort. The organization may elect to circumvent them by supplementing its internal resources with an external consultant.

In our view, an external consultant in the role of transformation leader is essential in terms of facilitating the effort, providing perspective, overcoming inertia, conducting team building with the reengineering team(s), and otherwise contributing to the success of reengineering.

In choosing a consultant, the organization must concentrate not only on experience, but also on the individual's personal chemistry with the organization. An external consultant with extensive, successful experience in reengineering brings many useful skills, qualities, and resources to the organization's effort:

♦ A sense of perspective.

♦ Knowledge of appropriate tools and benchmarks.

♦ An understanding of what must be done during reengineering and how to structure the effort.

♦ The energy and commitment necessary to complete reengineering.

♦ An established reputation.

♦ Exposure to a wide range of organizational situations, events, and activities.

♦ Resources that can be used to minimize the learning curve among staff members and to increase their initial credibility and productivity.

♦ Objectivity as a result of being unencumbered by organizational history, culture, and politics.

♦ The ability to make difficult recommendations.

Just as there are potential problems associated with an exclusively internal staff, so are there with one that's exclusively external. If the reengineering effort is simply outsourced to an external consultant and the organization abandons involvement, the results include no sharing of responsibilities with employees, no employee ownership of ideas, no employee sharing in the vision and the passion of the effort, and ultimately no employee commitment.

EMPLOYEE REACTIONS TO REENGINEERING

Human beings want security and stability, not change. Consequently, reengineering almost always meets resistance. People react to the change represented by reengineering with striking dissimilarity, across an entire spectrum of emotions. But most of them feel at least some degree of distress.

At the heart of their reactions may be any of several factors:

♦ An unwillingness to change.

♦ A lack of understanding about why change must occur.

♦ An organizational bias about certain practices and people.

♦ Fear of the unknown.

Reducing Resistance

Resistance can be reduced through the exchange of information and feedback about the change, open and honest communication, understanding of the purpose for change, and a trusting and accepting environment.[4]

Often people feel that their livelihoods, careers, and hard-earned organizational titles are being threatened. Unfortunately, media commentary about the downsizings, increased work loads, and demotions that sometimes result from reengineering hasn't helped to abate people's fears.

FOUR EMPLOYEE FACTIONS

There are four factions among the employees of any organization undergoing reengineering:

- *Passive Proponents*—those who recognize the need to do things differently but are not sure that reengineering is the right way to go about it.
- *Active Proponents*—those who are actively involved in and supportive of the effort.
- *Neutralists*—those who aren't affected or interested.
- *Inhibitors*—those who are bound by tradition or who fear that their territorial domains will be threatened.

These factions influence the process of reinvention and must be managed effectively. For example, active proponents may be too enthusiastic and may create inflated expectations and intimidate the less enthusiastic; they may need to be coached to temper their behavior. Passive proponents need education and continual reassurance, while neutralists require a more subtle approach. Often passive proponents and neutralists may be won over by educating them, by requiring them to participate to a limited degree at first and then progressively increasing their involvement, and by giving them direct input into the reengineering process.

There is no single way of managing inhibitors or turning them into proponents. Each situation is different and each inhibitor is unique. Thus, we recommend using a variety of techniques:

- Conducting one-on-one meetings.
- Identifying and addressing each of an inhibitor's issues and objections.
- Actively listening to the concerns of the inhibitor.
- Educating the inhibitor about reengineering.
- Inviting the inhibitor to participate in the effort.

A lot of [our employees] came out of the '60s and '70s, and they're still capable of asking why and questioning the status quo. They're willing to change, but only if they understand why.

J. Randall McDonald

Unfortunately, there will always be some who will not respond to these techniques; in such situations nothing short of senior-management intervention will turn them around.

REINVENTION CHANGES WORK LIFE

Core Processes vs. Departments

The structure of the reinvented enterprise is entirely different from that of the traditional organization. It is essentially flat, not hierarchical; its essence is core processes and networked responsibilities, not separate departments with separate positions and duties. Overhead departments, such as finance, legal, and information technology, are collapsed into a shared-service function that is capable of supporting all aspects of the enterprise.

The organization may find that managers have an especially hard time with a flat structure. Many managers' experiences have taken place exclusively within the paradigm of the hierarchical organization. Consequently, they may have difficulty in letting go of their turf and concentrating instead on processes.

Passive Proponents

Characteristics

- Knows something must be done
- Unsure as to how to do something
- Mindful of change and can be cautious
- Will support proponents
- Can be lead to active proponency with demonstrated results

Reengineering Proponents

Characteristics

- Advocates and champions
- Chartered with project
- Performs reengineering
- Seeks approval through results
- Can be overly aggressive
- Can elevate expectations
- Can intimidate

Neutral

Characteristics

- Can be aloof and passive
- May be interested, but non-committal
- May be slow to embrace reengineering
- Could be easily swayed or persuaded
- May become apathetic
- May require senior leadership and intervention to "get going"

Inhibitors

Characteristics

- Skeptical and protective
- Resist change and challenges processes
- Can be political adversaries
- Will not cooperate or slow to cooperate
- Will attempt to discredit effort
- Usually requires direct senior leadership involvement

Level of Support

Level of Participation

The Four Factions

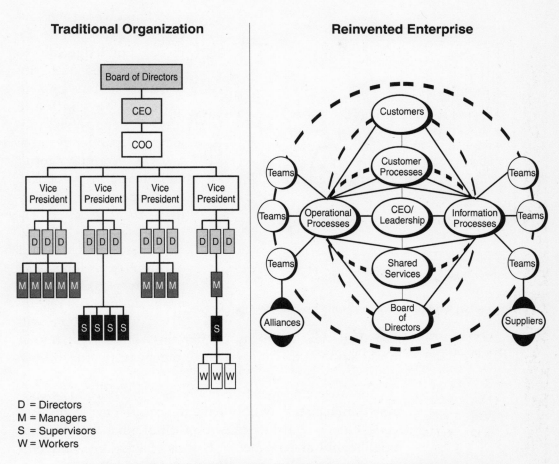

Traditional Organization

Board of Directors
CEO
COO
Vice President
Vice President
Vice President
Vice President
D D D
D D D
D D D
D D D
M M M M M
M M M
M
S S S S
S
W W W

D = Directors
M = Managers
S = Supervisors
W = Workers

Reinvented Enterprise

Customers
Teams
Teams
Customer Processes
Teams
Operational Processes
CEO/ Leadership
Information Processes
Teams
Teams
Shared Services
Teams
Alliances
Board of Directors
Suppliers

The Organizational Structure of the Reinvented Enterprise

Empowerment vs. Control

Because reinvention creates integrated processes, the need to control employees with multiple layers of management and checks and balances is eliminated. Organizational layers are compressed, and responsibilities are consolidated through increased employee productivity, enhanced technology, and empowerment.

"Stevens, get in here and give me some positive feedback."

Empowered employees are expected to be more knowledgeable, to have increased authority to make decisions, and are expected to challenge processes and solve problems independently or as a team. Nonmanagerial employees, in particular, may experience difficulty in assuming such expanded responsibilities. The organizational world of their experience has probably been much more neatly defined and restrictive. Although some will find their new authority exhilarating, others will find it intimidating and will need encouragement to stretch their abilities.

Because empowered employees don't have to be controlled, managers not only have to acquire new leadership skills, but also have to unlearn much of what they've been taught about management. They also have to measure employee performance according to new guidelines that emphasize employees' acquisition of knowledge, their creative use of technology, their personal productivity, and their use of expanded authority.

Skill Enhancement vs. Traditional Advancement

In the reinvented enterprise, traditional paths of advancement no longer exist. When the traditional organizational hierarchy is collapsed, the classical career progression disappears. The challenge for human resource professionals is to develop a course of cross-functional development, skills-enrichment opportunities, and rotational assignments for employees.

Advancement in the reengineered organization means:

♦ Being given greater responsibility for multiple processes.

♦ Acquiring greater knowledge of cross-functional structures and competitor practices.

♦ Developing the ability to identify breakthrough opportunities.

T raining programs are being used to enrich employees' skills at a time when the company can no longer offer lifetime employment or a predictable series of promotions.[5]

After reinvention both managerial and nonmanagerial employees are challenged and rewarded for continual innovation. Some will consider the new advancement system an improvement—especially the so-called "Generation X" employees, those born approximately from the mid-1960s through the late 1970s, who value gaining knowledge and skills more than they do traditional advancement. Others will lament the loss of the traditional career path and will need to be shown the advantages of the self-improvement path.

Centralized Authority vs. Teams

The ability of employees to function in a team environment is a prerequisite of reengineering and is one of the defining features of the reinvented organization. The team emphasis greatly reduces reliance on organizational titles and centralized authority.

In the reengineered organizational structure, organizational

Creating and Reinforcing Change

When the consultants move on and the process map comes down from the wall, the painfully won gains will leak away unless the employees who have to live with the new work design had a hand in creating it and unless the human systems of the company—compensation, career paths, training—reinforce the changes.[6]

behavior is based on self-directed work teams: These teams establish goals, solve problems, make decisions, and change practices. Members share responsibilities and distribute work among themselves.

This team orientation requires employees to work with others cooperatively, to participate actively, and to assume different roles as needed. Although the team approach has been used extensively in many organizations, it has rarely been relied on to the extent required by the reengineered organization.

Thus, employees will need training in making the transition from individually focused work to teamwork.

Background Leadership vs. Involved Leadership

A reengineering effort, unlike the situation in a traditional organization, depends on the direct participation and visibility of the executive leadership. In large reengineering projects that represent a high level of investment, business risk, and complexity, it's not uncommon for executives such as the CEO or COO to devote as much as ten to twenty percent of their available time.

This demonstrated commitment gives employees a chance to be involved with top leaders in a way that they may never have experienced. Such top-leadership participation not only reinforces the objective of achieving breakthrough results, but also helps employees to realize that their contributions to reengineering are seen as vital.

How Leaders Can Empower Others

Empowering others is essentially the process of turning followers into leaders. Leaders realize that they can empower others without diminishing their own power. The process of empowering others is facilitated when people work on tasks that are critical to the organization's success, when they exercise discretion and autonomy in their efforts, when their accomplishments are visible and recognized by others, and when they are well connected to other people of influence and support.[7]

CONCLUSION

Reengineering requires employees to abandon old behaviors and embrace new ones. Changing behavior can be challenging and, at times, painful.

Education and training must be provided, and mechanisms that foster new behavior must be in place. Communication must be increased and technology used so that people have easy access to whatever information they need.

In reengineering, the employees are asked to embark on an arduous journey. The organization must be supportive every step of the way.

In an article in Quality Digest, *Bob Mann says that the answers to today's business problems will not be found in the processes, behaviors, and thinking of the past. After all, he claims, those processes and behaviors, along with that thinking, created the very environment we strive to change today. We need new and innovative process-oriented behavior. This new behavior will enable orgainzations and people to keep pace with the present and to prepare for the future.*[1]

REVIEW:
TIPS FOR A
SUCCESSFUL JOURNEY

*The challenge is to pursue our vision with as much courage and
intensity as we can generate.*

Peter Block, writing in *The Empowered Manager*

10

Let's assume that the decision to reengineer has been
made. The organization has analyzed its situation; evaluated
its needs; and concluded that the reengineering journey will
help lead to operational excellence, greater competitive advantage, and enhanced shareholder value.

When your organization decides to reinvent itself and
embarks on reengineering, it will encounter unanticipated
issues, unresolved details, and setbacks. The challenge of
reengineering is accepting that it involves a continual cycle
of overcoming obstacles, refining processes and procedures,
and adapting as necessary. As we have discussed elsewhere
in this book, there are some ways to ease the journey, and in
this chapter we offer a review of these methods in the form
of tips.

Examine a Third World jungle culture or a corporate culture and certain characteristics are remarkably similar. Each has its leaders, heroes, stories, rituals, ceremonies, and artifacts. Each has deeply ingrained behavioral patterns that influence the way things get done.[2]

Reengineering gives rise to a deep psychological change. It starts with a bold vision, courageously pursued. That vision generates new behaviors, which, in turn, engender new leaders and heroes and stories—and, ultimately, a new culture.

Tip 1: Have a vision that's concrete, inspiring, and achievable. Everyone involved in the reengineering effort should understand the vision, be able to rally behind it, and know that it can be accomplished.

Tip 2: Make sure that top management supports reengineering. The CEO and COO must be totally committed to the process, and this commitment requires time and effort beyond approval to go ahead with reengineering.

Tip 3: Don't embark on reengineering in the context of a particular problem to be solved. Reengineering cannot be used in a narrow context or as a quick fix to a problem.

Tip 4: Use a proven methodology. Never initiate a reengineering effort without a meticulously designed methodology and a detailed work plan.

Tip 5: Don't look to information technology as the answer. Technology should not be the solution or the impetus for reengineering.

Tip 6: Don't depend solely on internal resources. Issues that are critical to the organization's mission, technically complex, or politically sensitive need the intervention of external resources.

Tip 7: Never attempt to reinvent the organization with a novice reengineering team. Experience with the process is essential.

Tip 8: Constantly challenge the findings, conclusions, and recommendations of everyone involved in reengineering. Always explore and evaluate all possibilities and alternatives. Striving for innovation is a never-ending proposition.

Tip 9: Try to create a balance between urgency and patience. Understand the implications of reengineering activities, and anticipate the reactions of the organization, the customers, and any business partners.

Conclusion

Organizations are not only at the threshold of a new century, but also at a new stage of evolution. As many have discovered, the tried-and-true management practices that once led to greatness are no longer appropriate in a world of increasingly greater competition and borderless economies.

To many organizations, it may seem that the best way to approach such monumental change in the environment is to play it safe and avoid risk. However, failure to recognize the need for internal change in response to external change will only lead to a further diminishment of the organization's capabilities, competitive posture, and shareholder value.

The choice is clear: Reengineer and flourish, or fail to reengineer and perish. Equally important is the benefit to those who participate in reengineering: Reinvention provides the opportunity to look into the mirror, explore what you find, and grow. For in the final analysis, to reengineer an organization, you must reengineer yourself.

Notes

Chapter 1

1. Adapted from R. Katz, "Is Reengineering Already Dead?," *Quality Digest,* Jan. 1995, p. 64.
2. Adapted from *PC World,* July 1993, p. 55.
3. *1993 Chrysler Financial Annual Report.*
4. Copyright 1993 by Computerworld, Inc., Framingham, MA 01701. Reprinted from *Computerworld.*

Chapter 2

1. Adapted from B. Filipczak, "Weathering Change: Enough Already!," *Training,* Sept. 1994, p. 29.
2. Adapted from R.K. Denton & C. Boyd, *Did You Know? Fascinating Facts and Fallacies About Business,* Prentice-Hall, Englewood Cliffs, NJ, 1994, p. 160. (Originally in "American Workers Are Overworked?," *APICS—The Performance Advantage,* May 1992, p. 10.)

Chapter 3

1. Adapted from J. Farrell, "A Practical Guide for Implementing Reengineering," *Planning Review,* March/April 1994, p. 45.
2. R. Eaton, CEO of Chrysler Corporation.

Chapter 4

1. Adapted from J.M. Kouzes & B.Z. Posner, *Leadership Practices Inventory (LPI): Trainer's Manual* (1994 ed.), Pfeiffer & Company, San Diego, CA, 1994, pp. 4–5.
2. *Computerworld,* May 3, 1993, p. 125.
3. G. Hall, J. Rosenthal, & J. Wade, "How to Make Reengineering *Really* Work," *Harvard Business Review,* Nov.–Dec. 1993, p. 130.
4. C.W. Wick & L.S. Leon, *The Learning Edge,* Wick and Company, Wilmington, DE, 1993.
5. Adapted from G. Dessler, "Value-Based Hiring Builds Commitment," *Personnel Journal,* Nov. 1993, p. 101.

Chapter 5

1. Adapted from K. Kelly, "Who Says Big Companies Are Dinosaurs?," *Business Week,* July 25, 1994, pp. 15–16.
2. B. Smith, quoted by D. Altany, "Copycats," *Industry Week,* Nov. 5, 1990, p. 18.
3. D. Altany, "Copycats," *Industry Week,* Nov. 5, 1990, p. 11.
4. F.G. Tucker, S.M. Zivan, & R.C. Camp, "How to Measure Yourself Against the Best," *Harvard Business Review,* Jan.–Feb. 1987, p. 8.

Chapter 6

1. Adapted from J. Greenwald, "Is Mr. Nice Guy Back?," *Time,* Jan. 27, 1992, p. 43.
2. "Becoming a Major Force," *Human Resource Executive,* Aug. 1994, p. 24.

3. Excerpted with permission of *DATAMATION* Magazine, Aug. 1, 1993, © 1993 by Cahners Publishing Company.

4. Adapted from *Nation's Business*, Feb. 1994, p. 21.

5. D. Bagin & F. Grazian, "Let's Employ Their Brains Too," *Communication Briefings*, June 1994.

CHAPTER 7

1. Adapted from A. Downs, "Planned People Obsolescence," *Training*, Feb. 1995, p. 57.

2. Adapted from "Middle Managers Sabotage TQM," *Training*, Sept. 1994, p. 85.

3. Adapted from K.L. Murrell & J.F. Vogt, "The Manager As Leader in an Empowering Organization," *The 1991 Annual: Developing Human Resources*, Pfeiffer & Company, San Diego, CA, 1991, pp. 299-300.

4. Adapted from B. Filipczak, "Weathering Change: Enough Already!," *Training*, Sept 1994, p. 26.

5. Adapted from "Walking in Your Customers' Shoes," *Training*, Feb. 1995, p. 16.

CHAPTER 8

1. Adapted from M. Michalko, quoted in *Communication Briefings*, Feb. 1995, p. 1. (Originally in *Training & Development*.)

2. D.C. Kielson, writing in *THE FUTURIST*. Courtesy of the World Future Society, Bethesda, MD.

CHAPTER 9

1. Adapted from B. Geber, "Preaching the Gospel," *Training*, Feb. 1995, p. 48.

2. G. Hall, J. Rosenthal, & J. Wade, "How to Make Reengineering *Really* Work," *Harvard Business Review*, Nov.-Dec. 1993, p. 131.

3. M. Loeb, "Where Leaders Come From," *Fortune*, Sept. 19, 1994, p. 242.

4. A.G. Henkel, C. Repp-Bégin, & J.F. Vogt, "Empowerment-Readiness Survey," *The 1993 Annual: Developing Human Resources*, Pfeiffer & Company, San Diego, CA, 1993, p. 147.

5. "Becoming a Major Force," *Human Resource Executive*, Aug. 1994, p. 24.

6. T.A. Stewart, "Reengineering: The Hot New Managing Tool," *Fortune*, Aug. 23, 1993, p. 48.

7. J.M. Kouzes & B.Z. Posner, *Leadership Practices Inventory (LPI): Trainer's Manual* (1994 ed.), Pfeiffer & Company, San Diego, CA, 1994, p. 5.

CHAPTER 10

1. Adapted from B. Mann, "Empowerment: An Enabling Process," *Quality Digest*, Jan. 1994, p. 43.

2. S. Greengard, "Reengineering: Out of the Rubble," *Personnel Journal*, Dec. 1993, p. 48K.

Index

THE WARREN BENNIS EXECUTIVE BRIEFING SERIES

*"To survive in the 21st century, we're going to need
a new generation of leaders, not managers.
This series is an exciting collection of business books
written to help your leaders meet the challenges of the new millennium."*

Dr. Warren Bennis
USC Professor and Founding Chairman, The Leadership Institute
Author, *On Becoming a Leader* and *An Invented Life*

Tailored to the needs of busy professionals and authored by subject matter experts, the *Warren Bennis Executive Briefing Series* helps leaders acquire significant knowledge in the face of information overload. All *Series* titles utilize the SuperReading comprehension/retention editing and design techniques made famous by Howard Berg, *The Guinness Book of World Records'* "World's Fastest Reader." Read these books in just two hours!

TITLES INCLUDE:

Fabled Service: Ordinary Acts, Extraordinary Outcomes	Betsy Sanders
The 21st Century Organization: *Reinventing Through Reengineering*	Warren Bennis/ Michael Mische
Managing Globalization in the Age of Interdependence	George Lodge
Coach to Coach: Business Lessons from the Locker Room	John Robinson
The Faster Learning Organization: *Gain and Sustain the Competitive Edge*	Bob Guns
The Absolutes of Leadership	Philip Crosby
Customer Inspired Quality: *Looking Backward Through the Telescope*	James Shaw
INFORelief: Stay Afloat in the InfoFlood	Maureen Malanchuk

Contact your local bookstore for all *Warren Bennis Executive Briefing Series* titles, or order directly from Jossey-Bass Publishers, Customer Service Department, 1-800-956-7739, 350 Sansome Street, San Francisco, CA 94104. For special sales or bulk purchases, call Bernadette Walter at 415-782-3122.